T0248273

Shari Lewis and Lamb Chop

Shari Lewis and Lamb Chop

The Team That Changed Children's Television

Nat Segaloff and Mallory Lewis
Foreword by David Copperfield

Published by The University Press of Kentucky, scholarly publisher for the Commonwealth, serving Bellarmine University, Berea College, Centre College of Kentucky, Eastern Kentucky University, The Filson Historical Society, Georgetown College, Kentucky Historical Society, Kentucky State University, Morehead State University, Murray State University, Northern Kentucky University, Spalding University, Transylvania University, University of Kentucky, University of Louisville, University of Pikeville, and Western Kentucky University.

Editorial and Sales Offices: The University Press of Kentucky
663 South Limestone Street, Lexington, Kentucky 40508-4008
www.kentuckypress.com

Unless otherwise noted, photographs are from the collection of Mallory Lewis and her family.

Library of Congress Cataloging-in-Publication Data

Names: Segaloff, Nat, author. | Lewis, Mallory, author. | Copperfield, David, writer of foreword.
Title: Shari Lewis and Lamb Chop : the team that changed children's television / Nat Segaloff and Mallory Lewis ; foreword by David Copperfield.
Description: Lexington : The University Press of Kentucky, [2022] | Includes index.
Identifiers: LCCN 2022011716 | ISBN 9780813196268 (hardcover ; acid-free paper) | ISBN 9780813196275 (pdf) | ISBN 9780813196282 (epub)
Subjects: LCSH: Lewis, Shari. | Puppeteers—United States—Biography. | Ventriloquists—United States—Biography. | Businesswomen—United States—Biography. | Lamb Chop (Fictitious character) | Children's television programs—United States.
Classification: LCC PN1982.L4 A48 2022 | DDC 791.5/3092—dc23/eng/20220329
LC record available at https://lccn.loc.gov/2022011716

This book is printed on acid-free paper meeting
the requirements of the American National Standard
for Permanence in Paper for Printed Library Materials.

Manufactured in the United States of America

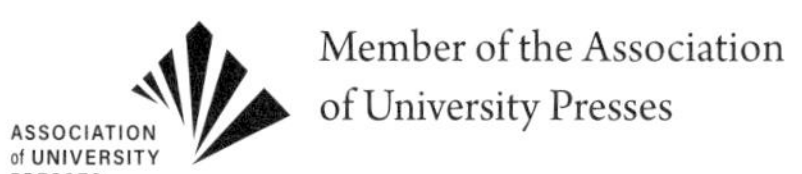

For Jamie; Grandma Shari loves you.
—*Mallory*

For Adam and Joseph Benjamin.
The future is yours, but honor the past.
—*Uncle Nat*

Contents

Foreword

I met Shari Lewis for the first time when I was a child in front of a very bright, smaller-than-normal tube. That TV screen is how we all met Shari Lewis for the first time. She was the perfect antidote for all the violence and shoot-'em-ups we'd seen on TV—a bit of calm with an amazing talent.

I didn't meet her in person until I was also on TV, and she was still a little untouchable because she was always working, always creating new things. But I knew her father, Abe Hurwitz, because he was "Peter Pan, the Magic Man," the "official" magician of New York City. Unlike a lot of the boys whom Doc Hurwitz took under his wing, I was not a troubled kid; I was more of a computer nerd, if they'd had those at the time. I found my niche in magic, although I started out as a ventriloquist; I remember watching her and her male counterpart, Paul Winchell. When I realized ventriloquism was not my calling, I shifted to magic.

Shari knew exactly who she was. She was someone who had invaluable training: theater, dance, music, singing, and she could act. A lot of young women could do that, but she found a way to make it her own; she found her own way. She also had an anchor in a father who got her lessons from John Cooper, the great African American ventriloquist. Abe made sure that his daughter had all the preparation she needed. She knew how to develop her character, which came from her relationship with those puppets. She started off with a classic wooden vent dummy but then, as we all do, she found her own way, in her case with the sock puppets. She and Lamb Chop had a special love for each other.

Watching her, I realized that sort of thing didn't exist in magic; magic was someone doing sleight of hand or using equipment, but what was missing, and which existed in every other form of entertainment, were relationships. But Shari figured that out. She knew how to make her relationship with that puppet integral to who she was. They became two people you could care about, and when the audience can relate, you've got them. Shari did that very well, eventually using it as a form to teach and inform and inspire. And that's what I want to do with my magic.

She was also technically brilliant. You believe what you are seeing. As with magic, you work hard to make it look effortless. She was one of the best, technically, but she had the wisdom of not stopping at that. She made the characters right for her.

Shari had something that was uniquely hers: the softness of the puppet. Lamb Chop, Charlie Horse, and Hush Puppy were huggable. Their voices were huggable. Shari Lewis was huggable! They were like a cup of hot chocolate. They made the audience feel comfortable, and if you can make the audience feel familiar, you've landed. Like Fred Rogers, she focused on what the medium of television could do. When you're doing things for kids—she wasn't only for kids, though mostly she was—what she'll be remembered for is being there for generations and generations of them—for surviving and keeping going, and she gave up a lot to do it.

She also—and what I try to do—gave people hope. How do you make people see possibilities that go beyond all the things they have in their lives? With me it's about future possibilities. With her it's about a song that never ends.

—David Copperfield

David Copperfield built a reputation on making the impossible look easy. He single-handedly redefined his art and remains the most emulated illusionist in the history of magic.

Preface and Acknowledgments

Once upon a time there was a woman whose life was a TV show. No matter where you looked, she was always onscreen somewhere, and over the years, she seemed to change more often than the channel. On one broadcast she was a dancer, on another a singer or an orchestra conductor, and on yet another an actress. She was also a rare thing for the time: a female ventriloquist. She commanded a zoo full of huggable heroes, but her (and the public's) favorites were a sassy lamb, a southern dog, and a self-assured horse, all of whom talked back. Shari Lewis, with the help of Lamb Chop, Hush Puppy, and Charlie Horse, raised three generations of children, including a daughter of her own. But if any of this cute and fuzzy stuff makes her sound saccharine, forget it.

Shari was a hot ticket. She was a dynamic, versatile, talented, focused, inventive entertainer who broke down doors and constantly found new doors to open when old ones started to close. She headed her own television company in an era when few women were employed in middle management in the broadcast industry, let alone at the top. Finally, as a beloved performer, she left a legacy of memories that can still make her now-grown-up fans smile and sometimes cry.

Yet for all her popularity with audiences worldwide, Shari was essentially a loner. Typecast as a ventriloquist despite having half a dozen other skills, she fervently tried to broaden her career, until at last she came to embrace her notoriety. Leaning into her gift for communicating with children, she became an educator as well as an entertainer. "Edutainment" is what she called it (years before others bent the term to suit their own ambitions), and she perfected it, earning award after award for her achievements.

Shari Lewis's story is one of persistence; her singular goal was to stay on television. Although success came early, she somehow knew that it was only ephemeral, and her life became a struggle to retain it. What it cost her and how it affected those around her are what this book is about. It's also about what she achieved. Her life, which lasted only sixty-five years, and her career, which lasted nearly as long, are lessons in survival and reinvention and also an inspiration for future innovators.

The authors of this book first came together in 1994 to chart that survival. Nat Segaloff was asked by Weller/Grossman Productions in Los Angeles to produce "Shari Lewis and Lamb Chop" as an episode for the *Biography* series on the Arts & Entertainment Network (now A&E). At the time, Mallory Lewis was known as Mallory Tarcher, the daughter of Shari and Jeremy Tarcher, and was working on her mom's TV series *Lamb Chop's Play-Along* and, later, *The Charlie Horse Music Pizza*. Mallory not only appeared in Nat's documentary but became a friend. After Shari died in 1998, Mallory picked up Lamb Chop and assumed her mother's professional name of Lewis. For reasons neither Mallory, Nat, nor Lamb Chop can explain, it took the three of them twenty years to stumble upon the obvious idea of writing this book.

This is not a standard biography. Because Shari, through her puppets, spoke in several voices, the authors decided that this book should too. In addition to traditional quotes embodied in the narrative, Mallory (and, on occasion, others) will tell side stories and stand-alone anecdotes in the form of sidebars. It will be like pausing a video to hear someone else in the room fill in a fascinating blank.

There have been many threads in the knitting of *Shari Lewis and Lamb Chop*: There's the way Shari discovered her "inner lamb." There's the truth behind Hush Puppy's personality. There's where the original Lamb Chop lives. There's the story of how Shari wrote a *Star Trek* episode as an "on camera" vehicle for herself and then got forced off her own script. There's Lamb Chop's memorable testimony before a congressional committee, and there are many other adventures. There are even some of Shari's favorite lamb recipes.

The legacy of Lamb Chop continues through Mallory, who performs all over the world with her mother's fabled hand puppet. In her act, she does something that her mother never did: she brings parents as well as kids up onstage. As she and Lamb Chop do their act, the tears flow, not from the kids but from parents who joyfully remember Shari from when they were young. Many grown-ups of a certain age admit that, as their families grew apart, Shari was the only adult friend they had. Grown men will blushingly confess that they had a teenage crush on her, and grown women will say that they drew strength from seeing a woman in charge.

Shari's impact on American television was profound. It worked on both individual and institutional levels. Perhaps therein lies the secret of her fame and why maintaining it was such a struggle. She had the ability to relate to people one-on-one, yet the television industry failed to see the importance of this gift, and she had to spend much of her time proving her talent to people who had none. Fortunately, many who saw her talent and loved her for it contributed their memories to this biography. The authors gratefully express their thanks to the people quoted in these pages and to (alphabetically) Jean Louise Codianni, Casey Compton, Brian Cummings, Lisa D'Apolito, Joe Giangrasso, Talley Wilmnot Hutcherson, Kate Cooper Jensen, Pamela A. Perry, Mary Anne Roberto, Adrienne Crane Ross, Jerry Ross, Ed Salier, Susan Swope, and Robb Weller, and to the Hurwitz family one and all.

Shari and American television share a history. For half a century they influenced one another, adapted their methods to meet new challenges, and shaped the field of children's programming. Then they were forced apart by a changing marketplace and set their sights on increasingly divergent goals, coming together when they were able to share those goals. Shari's is the story of children's television, perhaps the most abused arm of the most powerful mass communications medium the world has ever known. She was there from the beginning and never forgot its sacred promise to young people and the importance of keeping it.

When Shari performed, she may have created a fantasy world, but she didn't live in one. Always in charge, ever the realist, there's a story that illustrates the point. It happened during a preproduction conference on the first season of *Lamb Chop's Play-Along* when the male director, whom Shari didn't like, studied the physical layout of the soundstage and started looking for electrical outlets. "Where's the power in this studio?" he asked petulantly. Shari looked him in the eye and said, pointing at herself, "Right here, buster, right here."

Mallory Lewis and Lamb Chop

Dear Reader,

First and foremost I'd like to thank you for your continued interest in my mom. As I travel the country performing with Lamb Chop, I am always greeted with the kindness and love (from family and strangers alike) that Mom engendered over her sixty-plus years in the public eye.

That is why I wrote this book. I wanted to introduce Mom's fans to the "true Shari" (insofar as anyone ever truly knows anyone)—the *woman,* not just the *star.*

Mom was so much more than the "nice little lady with the puppet" or a "children's entertainer." She was so much more than an entertainer in general. More than an author. More than a conductor. More than a talk-show guest or a Vegas performer. Mom was a real-life, 3-D, fully developed woman. She was a mom (obviously), a pet lover, a wife, a daughter, a friend, a student, an athlete, an adventurer, and an activist.

Mom, like all people, had many ups and downs, although fewer of the latter than many. She had hopes, dreams, successes, failures, passions, and desires. And she loved a good "dirty" joke.

Often we pigeonhole public figures. In doing so we miss *so* much and do them and ourselves a disservice by not seeing them as fully human, with all the good and bad that goes with that. Mostly we miss the "interesting."

So thank you for taking the time to delve deeper into the life of my very interesting, super-fun mommy!

And now, with no further ado, I have the honor of presenting—my mom—Miss Shari Lewis!

Mally Lewis +

1

Born in a Magician's Trunk

If Abe Hurwitz had been able to pull his daughter out of a hat instead of having his wife give birth to her the regular way, he would have been the happiest magician in all of New York City. But no, the infant arrived in the traditional manner on January 17, 1933, and Abraham Benjamin Hurwitz and Ann Ritz Hurwitz named her Phyllis Naomi. The name was, to all accounts, the only downside of her childhood. She entered the world as the Great Depression was hitting bottom and the country was two months away from the inauguration of Franklin Roosevelt, who had been elected the previous November 8 on a platform of renewing America's economic promise.

But though times in general were tough, Ann and Abe had the advantage of having steady work. Ann was music coordinator for the Bronx school system and taught piano privately on the side. Abe was a part-time director of recreation at New York City's Department of Parks, but his main job was professor of recreation and physical education at Yeshiva University in Upper Manhattan. With this latter position came living quarters in one of the school's dormitories, and it was to these underwritten accommodations that "Doc" Hurwitz and his wife brought baby Phyllis home from the hospital.

The choice of Phyllis as her given name is a mystery. The tradition among Ashkenazi Jews is to name a child in honor of a deceased relative, but family trees stretching back to the old country suggest nothing close to either Phyllis or Naomi. Abe,[1] born in Kauvna, Lithuania, which was then part of Russia, was the son of Sarah (Jaffe) and Rabbi Benjamin

1. His birth date is unclear. Shari says he came to America in 1903, but his obituary (he died in 1981) says he was seventy-six, which means he was born in 1905 and must have

Joseph Hurwitz. His family, of which he was one of eight surviving siblings, was part of the great immigrant flood at the turn of the twentieth century.[2] Ann Ritz was born in New York in 1908, the daughter of Morris and Gussie Ritz, who were descended from Ritzes and Haftlers. Shari's grandfather Morris's parents were named Pola and Natan, which might account for Phyllis and Naomi, at least as far as the initials, but that's pushing it.[3]

> My memory of my great-grandmother Gussie Ritz is that she wore all black and spilled hot coffee on me once when I was two years old. That's it for me and Gussie: she looked like a crow and spilled hot coffee on me.
>
> —*Mallory*

Despite being descended from a family of rabbis, Abe, once he married Ann, observed just enough religious tradition to mollify their Yeshiva landlord. Jewish holidays among the Hurwitzes were followed casually at best, and the family considered themselves assimilated. While the Hurwitzes and their children neither denied nor renounced their Judaism, it did not play a significant part in their lives. "It was all done with mirrors," says cousin David Brown. "Abe had to act like he was Conservative because he was at the Yeshiva and that's Orthodox, but when we left the house they actually took me for my first Chinese meal."

If there was any abiding belief in Abe's life, it was magic. Taking the name Peter Pan the Magic Man, he performed in a green costume and drew upon a seemingly endless supply of mechanical illusions that he stored in every corner of their tiny apartment. Unlike amateur magicians who insist on doing card tricks for bored relatives and other captive audiences, by all accounts, Abe was both gifted and generous with his

---

come to America later. She also says he was born in Hercegovina, but a family history says Kauvna.

2. Panel 199 on the Ellis Island Wall of Honor names Benjamin J. Hurwitz. It was donated by his daughter Lillian Hurwitz Brown.

3. GENi Genealogical Search (www.geni.com); David Brown and Ben Brown, *LAHAB, 50th Anniversary Commemorative Book* (privately published, 1985).

Grandpa loved bacon. When asked why he, an ostensibly religious Jew, would eat *trayfe* (non-kosher food), he insisted, "I don't eat *pork*. Bacon is *not* pork."

—*Mallory*

talent. His theory, which was then revolutionary, was that people learn more easily when they're being entertained, and this led him to take a succession of young people, mostly wayward boys, under his wing to teach them math, chemistry, and other subjects through magic.

"I remember Daddy, at one of the Juvenile Halls, teaching a group of children how to pull money out of the air," Phyllis[4] wrote in 1975. "A tough youngster came up to him at the end of the lesson and assured him that he loved magic, and that pulling money out of the air was even easier than stealing it."[5]

My father was a terrific iconoclast. He was much more interested in boys than girls; he didn't have a son, so I became his son, and that was lucky for me. During the Depression he found that boys were not paying attention to the teacher, but they paid attention to a magician, so he learned his magic specifically for that purpose. I was brought up believing that education and laughter, facts and fun, education and entertainment were one and the same. My father would teach math magic and chemistry magic, and Mother knew way ahead of her time what they're now discovering, which is that music teaches you how to learn. Plato said, "I will teach the children physics, philosophy and music, and the most important of the three is music because the key to all learning lies in the path of the arts." What they're now discovering is that the synapses set up by music instruction are the key to all learning. Music is left brain; it only shifts over to the right brain when it becomes artistry.

—*Shari*

4. As we know, Phyllis Naomi Hurwitz would become Shari Lewis. For now, however, let's hold to chronology, except where Shari herself or an interview subject uses *Shari*.

5. Shari Lewis and Abraham B. Hurwitz, *Magic for Non-Magicians* (New York: Signet Classics, 1975).

Abe was a teacher first and a magician second. "Many years ago, working with problem children in New York, I saw a magician performing for a group of my delinquent boys," he wrote. "I was envious of the attention they had given to him but to no other teacher or leader. I saw that his magic had a power that could be employed in working with those boys so I, too, became a magician. For over forty years I have practiced my craft as teacher and camp leader, playground director, [and] orphanage administrator. That was a magical decision for me and I will always consider it the best one I ever made."[6]

Abe had a spectacular bent for children. He could control the worst child that ever lived in five seconds. He was amazing with children. He had a house filled with electric saw players, owls, rabbits—nonsense, because he believed in nonsense. He believed you could teach through nonsense. He used the word *nonsense:* "I'm gonna teach you some nonsense."

—Lan O'Kun

My funniest memory of Grandpa is that he would carry around this huge hankie and "use" it to blow his nose again and again. Then he'd pull it out of his pocket and say, "I'm going to show you a magic trick: here, hold this!"

—Mallory

Abe's reputation was such that, in 1937, when Phyllis was four, New York mayor Fiorello LaGuardia designated Abe "Doc" Hurwitz the Official Magician of New York City. The appellation "Doc" might have involved a little prestidigitation too. Although newspaper accounts say he received a master's degree from Columbia University and a doctorate in educational guidance from New York University, no one in the family can recall an official academic history. An alternate version offered by his kin is that when Abe began teaching at Yeshiva University in 1928, his job

6. Lewis and Hurwitz.

included supervising the medical students' dormitory, where the young men there affectionately called him "Doc." This makes a nice story until one remembers that Yeshiva didn't form a partnership with the Albert Einstein College of Medicine for another twenty years. Nevertheless, the nickname followed him throughout his career, although he used it more discreetly when it came to coauthoring several teaching books.[7]

Abe's wife, Ann, may not have found the truth so charming. "I don't think she was terribly happy," Mallory observed. "My grandfather told her he was a doctor and she didn't find out he wasn't until after they got married. That was the story. There was some other story. She was elegant, or she thought she was elegant, at any rate. And my grandpa was boisterous and so I think he annoyed her no end. I think she was angry about this until they both died."

If Abe was the magic, Ann was the music. As music coordinator, her job was to train other teachers in the public school system. Arts instruction was valued in those days, but it was rare at the time for a woman to hold a managerial position. Ironically, her lessons were lost on her own family, none of whom took up her cherished piano. Ann may have felt constrained by her husband's public persona and his penchant for inviting people—some of them barely above the level of stranger—over to the house. At times the foot traffic resembled vaudeville auditions as vagabond performers made the schlepp to Doc's place to reminisce about life in front of the footlights. Phyllis might have been enamored, but Ann watched the competition stoically, waiting her turn to blossom. "Nothing would have pleased Grandma more than to have been a school principal," her granddaughter Mallory says, "but she didn't have the time because she always had to be home to put dinner on the table."

7. Abe's books include *Games Children Play: Instructive and Creative Play Activities for the Mentally Retarded and Developmentally Disabled Child* (with Manny Sternlicht) (New York: Van Nostrand Reinhold, 1981); *Number Games to Improve Your Child's Arithmetic* (with Arthur Goddard and David T. Epstein) (New York: Funk & Wagnalls, 1975); *More Number Games: Mathematics Made Easy through Play* (with Arthur Goddard and David T. Epstein) (New York: Funk & Wagnalls, 1976); *Games to Improve Your Child's English* (with Arthur Goddard) (New York: Simon & Schuster, 1973); and *Magic for Non-Magicians* (with Shari).

Were Ann and Abe mismatched? "Maybe," Mallory says, "but there was also great love there. My grandfather was charming and a massive flirt. At one point Grandma got wind—or perhaps only imagined—that Grandpa was having an affair with the wife of the local butcher. She purposely left her umbrella in the butcher shop and sent my grandfather to fetch it, knowing that it would bring him face-to-face with the butcher. This was my grandmother's way of letting Abe know that she was onto him and that two could play at this game. I have no idea if she or he ever actually had an affair, but they were young and human so, probably, right?"

It was in this home—or, more significantly, in this environment—that baby Phyllis was raised. Almost immediately her parents started looking for a roomier place to live. The answer was a house on Staten Island, a quick ferry ride back to Manhattan for Doc's teaching duties. They were to live there until Parkchester, a 171-building planned community, opened in the East Bronx. Commenced in 1938 by the Metropolitan Life Insurance Company on a 129-acre plot originally owned by the New York Catholic Protectory (a school for troubled boys), the project was nearly put on hold when World War II consumed available construction materials. Parkchester was considered so essential, however (as were Manhattan's Riverton and Stuyvesant Town developments, which were planned at the same time), that building continued to completion in 1941. The first 500 units opened early in March 1940, and the Hurwitzes moved into the South Quadrant's 1505 Archer Road building.

The home was, quite literally, full of music and magic. "Abe was a collector of tricks," says his nephew Benjamin Brown, "particularly mathematical tricks, and he compiled a collection. His influence on Shari was

---

Mother and Daddy both constantly brought to dinner kids who needed a meal, needed a piano lesson, needed some guidance, needed some comfort, so we always had kids I didn't know at dinner. There were always a lot of magicians around. We had a very nice family, I must say. Mother was the kind of lady who made the graduation dress for a cousin who couldn't afford one.

—*Shari*

---

phenomenal. Both her parents influenced Shari. Dance lessons, singing lessons—they pushed her into being an entertainer and did a great job.[8] Obviously she learned a lot and had the talent and was at the right place at the right time. I always marveled." In 1958, adolescents Ben and his brother David spent a month living with the Hurwitzes when their parents, Lillian and Horace, went on adult vacation. Says Ben, "That's a month I remember almost every day of. I was a piano player. I spent a lot of time in their living room playing the piano and they encouraged me to continue to play morning, noon, and night. Abe took me under his wing and showed me what I believe was every box of magic he had in his house. I just ate it up. He did all forms of card tricks and number tricks; I can remember some of it to this day. They were both very, very good to us."

Most parents might have tried to dissuade their child from entering show business. The Hurwitzes encouraged it. They had Phyllis, at the age of four, performing with the band at Aunt Lillian and Uncle Horace Brown's wedding. "And she wouldn't do it unless I was with her, we were that close," says her cousin Harriet Ehrlich, who attended. "I got down on my hands and knees—I was her first partner and assistant—and we sang, 'On the Good Ship Lollipop.'"

Little Phyllis branched out from family functions when she accompanied her father, even before she hit her teens, in local USO shows. At times Abe would solicit bookings for his daughter; if he got $25 for a gig, he would nudge the producer and say, "Why don't you also hire my daughter?" and squeeze him for another $15.

"My father was remarkable," Shari recounted. (From now on, we'll refer to Phyllis as Shari, even though she didn't change her name until she was in her teens.) "He never put me in his act as his assistant, he never sawed me in half, he never asked me to help him set up his equipment. He gave me an act of my own. First it was three minutes and then it was ten and then it was twenty and then there was the day at the Lyric Theatre in Baltimore when I was fifteen when I did my twenty-minute act and they wouldn't let Daddy back on the stage. And he was so thrilled, like a leprechaun he jumped around. I was very lucky that Daddy didn't have a son. If he'd had a son, none of the good stuff would have happened to me."

8. Shari always said she started performing at the age of eighteen months.

The single condition Shari made in her budding career was that, after the Brown wedding, she refused to perform at family functions. It was, she said, the one difference between her and her father, who loved entertaining the kinfolk. Was she skeptical of the lenient applause she might earn from her gene pool, or was she simply saving her energy for paying audiences? She never explained it.

"Mom loved growing up in the Bronx," says Mallory. "She started at the age of three performing with my grandfather. At the age of nine he put her on a train with a trunk of tricks to Philadelphia, or wherever she was performing, and the JCC [Jewish Community Center] or the Temple at the other end would pick her up and she would perform and then they would send her home. This was an era—1942, during the war—when you could put a nine-year-old girl on a train."

"You must understand this house," explains Lan O'Kun, who would become Shari's brother-in-law and chief creative collaborator. "Doc was a wonderful man. I loved him dearly and he loved me dearly. He brought Shari up to be in show business. She learned all the parts of *nothing.* A little hoofing, the electric saw, dancing, the whole panoply of nothing, so that what she was, was a conglomeration of tiny talents. All of my writing life I had to write in her range so that she could sing whatever I wrote, and so forth. Shari was a conglomerate, a huge conglomerate."

Shari had nine and a half years alone in the spotlight by the time her sister, Barbara, was born on August 11, 1942. (There had been a miscarriage of a son in the years between the sisters' births.) Ann did not recover quickly from Barbara's delivery and had a hysterectomy, which meant that it fell to Shari to help raise her kid sister. She resisted, creating a tension and competitiveness that persisted throughout the girls' lives.

"All of this affected my sister more than it did me," Shari wrote. "She used to watch Pop make everything disappear and then say 'Abra Ca Dabra' and bring it all back, and it must have been frustrating to her. One day when she was about three we heard a loud noise from another part of the house. We ran toward it and found my sister standing over the john, dropping my mother's jewelry into it and saying 'Abra Ca Dabra' and pressing the handle! She made the jewelry disappear, all right, but even Daddy's magic couldn't bring it back."[9]

9. Lewis and Hurwitz, *Magic for Non-Magicians.*

The year 1942 was also when the family patriarch, Rabbi Benjamin Hurwitz, died suddenly, widowing Sarah. Thereafter, when the various Hurwitzes weren't gathered at Doc and Ann's, they would assemble at Sarah's home on Honeywell Avenue in the Bronx. Her emergence as matriarch conferred on her the title "Little Grandma."

Although Ann's and Abe's school posts were secure, they did not provide enough salary to put lamb on the table year-round. This meant

> The house on Honeywell Avenue was really the magnet that held the family together. My mother (Lillian Brown, Doc's sister) had some crazy stories she came up with that the Rockefellers owned that house and they gave it to the Rockefellers' butler or something. Beats the hell out of me. It was a fairly large home.
>
> —*Ben Brown*

that, like countless educators before and after, they had to take summer jobs. Abe found work as a counselor at a day camp in Mount Vernon, New York, while Ann took a similar position at a sleepover camp, Camp Crestwood, in Southington, Connecticut. Shari and Barbara joined her there, with Barbara, starting at age two, reluctantly consigned to the camp's Kiddie Kingdom auxiliary. Abe would visit Camp Crestwood on weekends to teach sports and perform magic, and his arrival made the arrangement a family affair. His niece Harriet Ehrlich, who was barely a teenager, rose to the challenge of helping Abe in his act. "I was his shill," she says proudly. "I would sit in the audience and when he would say, 'Who wants to come up?' I would say, 'I will!'"

It was at Camp Crestwood that Ann took the name Shari, which she said stood for "leader." "Maybe 'Aunt Ann' didn't sound euphonious enough," opined Elya Naxon, Shari's closest cousin. Biblically, "Shari" refers to someone from the Plain of Sharon in the Holy Land. In popular usage, it also means "song of God."[10] The real reason is more mundane.

10. It is also the Westernization of Sarah, the wife of Abraham in the Old Testament, meaning "mother of many nations." There is speculation that the spelling *Shari* was unknown before Lewis's rise to popularity. Prior to that, its closest variants were *Cheri, Sherry,* and *Sherree.*

"Because her name was Ann," Barbara says, "and the camp nurse's name was Ann, and the camp drama counselor's name was Ann—there were four or five Anns—my mother had worked at Camp Shari the year before and simply took the name Shari." Soon her older daughter did the same. Neither parent objected or, apparently, even remarked on it; it just sort of happened, and it stuck: the little girl who had been born Phyllis had been reborn as Shari. But the Hurwitz remained.

2

A Lucky Break

Camp Crestwood brought Shari into contact with two men who would shape her life. One was a counselor at the camp, the slightly older (by three years) Stan Lewis. The other was Saul Turteltaub, who attended the nearby boys' camp and visited two or three times a week. "We were boyfriend and girlfriend," says Turteltaub, who became one of television's most successful comedy writers (*That Girl; Love, American Style; Sanford and Son*), "although we didn't call it dating in those days. She would come to the dining room, I would come to the dining room, she would go back to the girls' camp, I would go back to the boys' camp, and I'd say, 'Ooh, what a good date that was.' We winked over prunes. And that was our relationship for that summer. We just liked each other; we were just good, good friends. Between the summers we didn't keep in touch," he continues. "We just occasionally would write a note because we lived in terrible guilt because she lived in the Bronx and I lived in New Jersey and I was too young to drive and I wasn't gonna take two buses and fourteen subways and have my passport renewed to go visit her every once in a while. I didn't see her in the city so I felt very guilty. We just dated that first summer, but we still liked each other; there was nothing not to like about her and there was nothing not to like about me, when I was fifteen; I was very nice as a fifteen-year-old kid."[1]

Stan Lewis was another matter. Born Stanley H. Lewis on April 21, 1930, to Harry and Florence Schaeffer Lewis of Brooklyn, he and Shari started dating at Camp Crestwood. He went out of his way to make young Barbara, who was twelve years his junior and stuck in the children's section, feel comfortable. "He was wonderful," Barbara recalls. "He was

1. Saul Turteltaub, interviewed in 1994.

really fun. Because my mother was head counselor at a camp, I had to be a good girl or I got killed. If there was a raid, I couldn't go on a raid, so the next night he'd take me out and we'd go on a rowboat on the lake, or we'd break into the dining room and we'd eat anything we wanted to so I could be a bad girl but not get into trouble. I was in Kiddie Kingdom from the time I was two until I was five or six."

Saul Turteltaub also got into the act. "He would pay attention to me because my mother was always busy," Barbara says. "He was a giant even then when he was only fifteen and I was a shrimp when I was five and he would carry me around on his shoulders."

But life is not all summer camp, and eventually Shari's professional drive kicked in. "I was out of the house by the time [Barbara] was four," she explained in a 1994 interview. "I've been working since the time I was fifteen years old, since I graduated from high school. I have always said that I was an only child and, if you don't believe me, you can ask my sister. She always felt that I abandoned her, because the minute I started working, I was out of the house. It's very hard to establish a beachhead in this business, and I knew that and really worked at it. But lately I have come to appreciate my sister and we have become closer than we ever were." Barbara agrees. "Did Shari resent having to take care of me?" she asks. "No. She was a very good older sister growing up."

The curtain was always rising at the Hurwitz home. Doc's outgoing personality and Ann's determination attracted a diverse menagerie of visitors: entertainers; scholars; cousins, nieces, and nephews; and neighborhood kids in need of guidance. The Parkchester apartment had three bedrooms: one for the parents, one for Barbara, and one for Shari. Everybody had to share space with Abe's magic tricks, a caged owl, and a

There was so much magic paraphernalia in the house that the only place for my grandparents to keep the rabbits—'cause you just aren't a magician without a rabbit or two—was in the bathtub. Mom told me they had to remember to close the toilet lid, or else the rabbits, as they tried to escape the tub, could jump out and land in the toilet and drown. From what she said, this was a semiregular occurrence.

—*Mallory*

bathtub full of rabbits ("which you had to clean every time you wanted to take a bath," Barbara remarks). The apartment was too small for family affairs, which could run to forty people, so for such occasions Abe secured space at Yeshiva University, where he taught until retiring in 1972.

No one in the Hurwitz clan ever doubted Shari's show business dreams or her parents' encouragement of them. Clearly she was following in her father's footsteps. But she was also blazing a trail that her mother had once hoped to follow. "When Ben and I were living there, I picked up a few tidbits," David said, recalling the brothers' 1958 stay. "One of them was that Ann thought she was going to be a concert pianist and Abe, for whatever reason, held her back and she resented it. There was this 'I coulda shoulda woulda' resentment going on."

> So here I am in Vietnam, I'm a dentist, and a kid comes in. He's a grunt, a private, and I'm working on his teeth and I say, "Where ya from?" "The Bronx." "Where in the Bronx?" "Parkchester." "You know Ann Hurwitz?" "Yes. She was wonderful." She was the music teacher, led the orchestra for the school, and she had good vibes. And this is just one guy. What can I tell you? Four or five months later, another guy from Parkchester spoke positively too. Kinda neat, huh? She was beloved by her students.
>
> —*David Brown*

It remained for Shari's music teacher at Herman Ridder Junior High School, Etta Morris, to help turn her toward professional training and the High School of Music & Art.[2] The only obstacle was the piano. Although Ann made her take piano lessons, Shari detested the instrument, and her playing confirmed it. Nevertheless, she had to make a go of keyboard to qualify for admission to Music & Art, as it was then known, so Miss Morris gave up her lunch hours to bolster Shari's proficiency, if not her passion. It was an ordeal, but it paid off.

Music & Art was a show business Mecca. Founded in 1936 near Amsterdam Avenue and 135th Street in Upper Manhattan, it was a magnet

2. Other notable Ridder graduates include Al Pacino, Hal Linden, and Regina Resnick.

I never liked the piano. The piano is not for me. I'm little; I was always little. You have to attack a piano. I got into Music & Art when I was eleven, they put a violin under my chin, and I found God! Sensual, it was musical! Once I got to the violin they couldn't stop me. But I didn't want to practice the piano. A child should be encouraged to listen to the very best of many instruments and to study one for six months and then switch. And eventually one of them will stick. It's like throwing something against the wall to see what sticks. The best is if you can play in groups. That's what Music & Art offered. That's the tragedy now that music education is being removed from the schools. Kids who studied music in schools, who get an instrument, those kids have better posture. Those kids have far better attendance. Those kids have a better attitude. Because music is a turn-on. What you learn from studying music is that you learn how to study anything. Music, you sit down and you don't know the first thing about what you're studying. And if you stick to it, WOW! what a piece of information.

—Shari

My mom told me a story about how she got into Music & Art. Her audition piece was "Flight of the Bumblebee" on the piano. She played it so fast that the lady for whom she was auditioning asked her, "Are you going to a fire?" Mom just wanted to hurry up so she could get to a dance lesson, which was much more to her liking.

—Mallory

school for talented children from the city's five boroughs. Admission practically ensured attention by agents and producers. Entry was strictly by audition, so to prepare Shari for hers, another teacher, Mrs. Rothstein, would drag her out of classes to read the Bible to her fellow students at school assemblies to give her public speaking experience. Finally, Syd O'Kun—Lan O'Kun's father and the founder and faculty sponsor of Ridder's school newspaper—took her off the student staff because he wanted her to focus her energies on entertainment rather than journalism.

There's a "ships passing in the night" story around this decision. Says Lan O'Kun, "I was fifteen and she was fourteen. Every few months the staff of that newspaper would meet at our house and my father taught them." When asked whether this was where he met Shari, O'Kun pointedly corrects, "No, it's where *she* met *me.* I lived there, and she was there. I was 'Mr. O'Kun's kid.'" Because Mr. O'Kun's kid didn't attend the same school as Doc Hurwitz's kid (Syd made Lan attend Macomb Junior High to avoid any potential nepotistic conflict of interest), the start of the decades-long Shari-Lan partnership would have to wait.

Shari began attending Music & Art in 1947 and graduated in 1950. Somehow, she says, she worked into her class schedule dance lessons at the American School of Ballet before beginning at Columbia University. College didn't last; she withdrew from Columbia after her first year to become a full-time performer.

> During Mom's tenure at Columbia she was the one inside the mascot costume at football games. I'm fairly sure it was the same costume three decades later when I attended Barnard.
>
> —*Mallory*

Of all the breaks Shari got during these early years, the most consequential was her leg. Occurring when she was a teenager and pursuing a dance career, it was such a turning point in her life that she frequently mentioned it when she gave interviews, carefully leaving out exactly how old she was when it happened.[3] "The story is that she wanted to be a dancer, she fell and broke her leg somehow, and while she was recuperating, to entertain her, they taught her magic," says cousin David, "and along with the magic came the ventriloquism, and along with the ventriloquism came the dummy."

Adds Elinore Brown, "Abe told me the story directly that he had a friend, a black guy who was a vaudevillian, a ventriloquist, and when Shari

3. A relatively contemporary *Newsweek* interview (July 14, 1958) says she was seventeen. At some point in her teen years she also had a nose job. In her later years, she underwent several skillful cosmetic surgeries.

I have read interviews where she says she broke her leg at seventeen, eleven, and assorted other ages. I think it made a good story but not necessarily an accurate one. Mom always told me that there was no way at five feet tall she was going to be a prima ballerina, and if she couldn't be a prima ballerina, she wasn't going to do it at all.

—*Mallory*

was holed up in the house and couldn't get around, he said, 'Go over to the house and teach her ventriloquism,' and he did." Cousin Bernice Zalk confirms, "That's when she learned about the ventriloquism. Abe had magicians and all sorts of show people coming to the house. While she was laid up in the house with her leg broken, one of them came in and he did the same work [with a puppet] and he started to teach her. Then she continued on her own and with Abe. That's the way she got her start."

"If I remember the story," says cousin Elya Naxon, offering more details, "her father said, 'You can't just lie there. I'm gonna bring somebody in to work with you,' someone who came in and taught her to be a ventriloquist. Just to keep her occupied. That's when she made the transition from dancing. I don't know how she broke her leg, but she was in bed and [Abe] got her a teacher."

None of these timelines makes much sense to me, as she was on TV by age seventeen doing ventriloquism, but the "you can't just lay there and do nothing" sounds exactly like my family.

—*Mallory*

Her ventriloquism teacher was most likely John W. Cooper (1873–1966), according to both the fan-based DreamWorks Wiki and the *Encyclopedia of Puppetry Arts;* the latter adds Monsieur Brunard (1901–1986) and Stanley Burns (1919–1998) to the list of her instructors and influences, but their names seldom turn up in her interviews or acknowledgments. Cooper was a major figure in American ventriloquism. An African American who crossed over from the Negro circuit to the white circuit during a white actors strike in 1901, he was the rare performer of color who was allowed to appear without "blacking up," a peculiar tradition in which African Americans were told to apply heavier blackface, adding insult to the injury of racism. By the 1920s he and his dummy "Sam Jackson" had been on *Major Bowes' Amateur Hour* and were touring Catholic churches. Cooper and Jackson's specialty was entertaining children, a calling that brought them into Doc Hurwitz's circle.

Monsieur Brunard, whose real name was Richard Bruno, started as a vaudeville musician but was inspired to become a ventriloquist after working with Cooper. Retiring from performing after World War II to stage children's shows for New York's Harmony Club, he easily joined the Hurwitz family. Stanley Burns, who lived and worked until 1998, is credited with being the first to use radio-controlled devices to liberate his puppets from his hand, starting with "Dr. Lichi" in the 1950s. He was a highly visible lecturer and author as well as a performer.

Such influences could not help but have inspired Shari during her recovery. At the very least, the broken leg—or perhaps it was just a sprain—gave her an excuse to stop pursuing dance, a career in which she knew she could never be a star. Even so, she kept dance in her broad repertoire and continued taking lessons throughout her life.

"I'll tell you the true story," says sister Barbara, smiling and launching into a correction of the legend. "It's such a good story that I don't know why people don't tell it, including Shari. She had the measles—she must have been seventeen-ish—and she was in bed. In our house we always had magicians and puppeteers and ventriloquists and belly dancers and that sort of group. At Yeshiva University there was this wimpy boy who had been drafted and he was having a nervous breakdown. He was the sole support of his mother. My father said to him, 'Don't have a nervous breakdown. I'm gonna make you into a magician and you're gonna stay in New York and will do special performances and will support your mother.' This wimpy kid couldn't even talk [in public], so my father did a whole silent magic act for him and, indeed, the kid went into Special Services. He had nothing [to pay with], so he gave my father the only thing he had, which was a 'Jerry Mahoney' doll.[4] There happened to be

4. Coming to prominence in 1938, Paul Winchell became known for his wisecracking Jerry Mahoney and dullard Knucklehead Smiff dummies. Winchell was also an inventor,

a ventriloquist at the house that day—they all hung around—and it was he who taught my sister how to be a ventriloquist." As an afterthought, she adds, "he later resented teaching Shari."

It was the dummy that kindled Shari's nascent talent. Ventriloquism is a blend of vocal agility and the magician's art of distraction. By turning her head toward her puppet as the puppet spoke, she more clearly mimicked the interaction of comedic partners onstage. A canny use of several techniques burnished her already remarkable skill.

I was walking by a closet and Daddy heard my sister screaming to be let out. He opened the door and my sister was nowhere to be seen. I had thrown my voice, and he thought this was just terrific.

—*Shari*

To disguise her first puppet's Mahoneyness, Shari placed a blond wig on its head, put it in a dress, gave it face paint, and renamed it "Taffy Twinkle." One of the stories Shari enjoyed telling is that, at first, she was not allowed to perform at Jewish community centers because Judaism forbids idol worship, and her vent dummy (as they are called)[5] was deemed to be an idol. Rather than spark a Talmudic scandal, Doc Hurwitz took a chisel and chipped an ear off the dummy underneath its wig and proclaimed, "Now it's a *defiled* idol!" making it acceptable. Shari also joked that Jewish dietary rules deemed rabbits to be non-kosher, so instead of pulling a rabbit out of a hat, she learned to whip out a chicken. Ever the opportunist, when the chance arose to make promotional appearances for a local bakery, Shari temporarily re-renamed Taffy Twinkle and called her "Buttercup," after the bakery's bread brand.

---

holding more than two dozen patents, including for components of the Jarvik-7 artificial heart. Winchell and Shari appeared together in a *Love, American Style* episode ("Love and the Dummies," December 1, 1969) in which two shy ventriloquists break the ice by speaking through their puppets.

5. *Vent* is derived from the Latin term for "speak from the stomach." It is the root of the word *ventriloquism*. By extension, a vent dummy is a ventriloquist's puppet.

It was at this stage that Shari set her sights on wider public exposure. Enough with the Lions Club and Hadassah luncheons. The best way to get noticed in New York in those days was *Arthur Godfrey's Talent Scouts.* There was just one problem, and it wasn't her talent. It was her name.

3

Becoming Lewis

Arthur Godfrey, who called himself the "Old Redhead," was a broadcast phenomenon. Though born in Manhattan, Godfrey—in both looks and manner—exuded the folksy, bucolic attributes that advertisers and magazine illustrators liked to think of as midwestern all-American. He talked slowly, played the ukulele, wore Hawaiian shirts (saying "Hawaya, Hawaya, Hawaya"), and gave the impression that everything on his show was there by his royal decree, which it was. Like so many others in show business, he was in the right place at the right time. While covering FDR's funeral procession in Washington, DC, for CBS Radio on April 15, 1945, his tearful and heartfelt benediction, "God bless him, President Roosevelt," moved millions of listeners, none more so than William S. Paley, the president of CBS.[1] Almost immediately, Godfrey was hired to host a daily ninety-minute morning network variety show called *Arthur Godfrey Time*. On July 2, 1946, he added the weekly thirty-minute *Arthur Godfrey's Talent Scouts* to his workload. In 1948 he moved *Talent Scouts* to CBS Television, running the audio track as a radio show and making no concession to the visual medium. In 1951 it hit number one in the ratings and would have stayed there the next season if *I Love Lucy* had not arrived. Until its cancellation in July 1958, *Talent Scouts* remained in the top ten.

No single broadcaster before or since has matched Godfrey's power. Unlike many of today's radio and television personalities, Godfrey realized that though people may listen in a group, each person hears as an individual. This epiphany not only made him an endearing emcee but

1. By contrast, on May 6, 1937, announcer Herb Morrison's career nearly ended when he vomited his horrified emotions ("Oh the humanity!") while reporting the *Hindenburg* disaster at Lakehurst, New Jersey.

also made him a successful commercial pitchman. When he endorsed a product, even if he made fun of it, housewives across America lined up to buy it. This power also made him egocentric and capricious.[2]

The gauntlet for *Talent Scouts* was remarkably uncomplicated in those days, before the payola scandal imposed rules on broadcast contests. Godfrey simply invited the public to recommend acts they had seen, while giving preference to people represented by his personal and professional contacts. Understandably, agents recommended their own clients, and parents pushed their children. The catch was that the contestants had to already be working in show business, even if they were relative unknowns; in other words, no amateurs need apply. The selectees then performed on the air, and the strength of the studio audience's applause determined the winner (by Godfrey's judgment).

By whatever contrivance, the system racked up a stunning record of success. Among its discoveries were Pat Boone, the McGuire Sisters, Carmel Quinn, Tony Bennett, Lenny Bruce, Roy Clark, Patsy Cline, Rosemary Clooney, Ken Berry, Wally Cox, Vic Damone, Eddie Fisher, Connie Francis, Don Knotts, Steve Lawrence, Al Martino, Barbara McNair, Johnny Nash, Leslie Uggams, and Jonathan Winters.

There was only one hitch: Godfrey was reputed to be a raging anti-Semite. Debated even today, the rumor was enough at the time to place Jewish performers such as Lenny Bruce (born Leonard Alfred Schneider) and Eddie Fisher (born Edwin Jack Tisch) on their guard, and it may have sent signals to the ethnically named Shari Hurwitz.

There is some uncertainty about what Shari did on *Talent Scouts*. Apparently, no recording exists. Did she perform with Taffy Twinkle? Did she, as she claimed in some accounts, sing Cy Coleman's "She's a

2. Readers of a certain age will remember that Godfrey famously fired his discovery, singer Julius LaRosa, live on the air on October 19, 1953. Godfrey told the audience, "That was Julie's swan song with us" and then lectured the shocked young man that he was being booted from the show because he had "lost his humility." A network cover story was quickly fabricated that LaRosa had asked to be released from his contract and Godfrey was merely wishing him well. It backfired, and Godfrey's star began to dim. He had become so dangerously influential that scriptwriter Budd Shulberg was inspired to pattern the charismatic and malevolent demagogue "Lonesome Rhodes" in *A Face in the Crowd*, Elia Kazan's 1957 film exposé of the power and deception of TV, in part on Godfrey.

Lady"? Whatever she did, it won her first prize and an offer for three more appearances on Godfrey's upcoming radio shows. Unfortunately, as she explained in later interviews, she had just the one routine she had performed on *Talent Scouts,* so with nothing else ready to go, she was helpless to object when Godfrey withdrew the booking. "My first victory brought me my first defeat," she said.[3]

> Other TV personalities of 1953, such as Mary Hartline [of *Super Circus*] and Roxanne [Delores Rosedale of *Beat the Clock*] may have been viewed as television's first sex goddesses, but Shari Lewis has earned a greater distinction in the decades since. She's become Saturday's only lasting love. From the first day she signed on the air, youngsters have seen her as the perky and sweet older sister, while adolescents have measured her against the girl next door. Colleagues, on the other hand, have looked beyond the beautiful blond locks and rosy cheeks and have been humbled by her talent and ability.
>
> —*Gary H. Grossman,* Saturday Morning TV

While Shari's professional life was idling, her personal life was going full speed ahead. She and Stan Lewis continued to see each other after their Camp Crestwood days. Stan was involved in the advertising industry, had acquired several clients, and began specializing in a new form of sales called "marketing," which fit his talents. "I don't know what you'd call it," says Lan O'Kun, chuckling at the memory. "Let's say there were potatoes and you wanted to sell the potatoes. He'd say to the producer of the TV show, 'I have these potatoes. If we put what's-his-name's name on them, we'll sell potatoes.' The man would say, 'We haven't got room for potatoes.' So Stan would stand on the side of the studio and, while the show was on television, he'd roll potatoes across the stage."

It was a crude, early form of product placement. The idea behind product placement is not just to associate a product with a person or event but to do it in such a way that the audience doesn't know it's being

3. Quoted by Gary H. Grossman in *Saturday Morning TV* (New York: Dell, 1981).

done to them, such as when a movie star orders a Coke in a restaurant scene or a Wonder Bread truck is parked on a street in the background.

"Stan was a hustler," says Barbara. "He spent many weekends with me because Shari was doing shows. He would take me to the movies, he would take me for Nathan's hot dogs, rides in convertibles, spare ribs, pizza, all the good things I was unexposed to as a child. He delighted in giving me a good time, and he did."

In plying this emergent trade, Stan Lewis overcame an obstacle that Shari had been burdened with from birth. Show business was largely Jewish, yet most Jewish performers Christianized their names to "pass." The advertising industry, in those *Mad Men* days, was not Jewish; in fact, it was practically anti-Semitic. With the buying public wallowing in the postwar economic boom of the 1950s, the advertising industry expanded rapidly, and Stan rose within it. But he had a secret: his family name was actually Lipshitz. Going forth as "Stan Lewis," he offered Shari an opportunity to dodge the cudgel of discrimination. Thus, when Stan H. Lewis (né Lipshitz) married Phyllis N. Hurwitz after Shabbat on Saturday, February 21, 1953, it offered a fresh start for each of them.[4] There is no indication that it was a big family wedding. Rabbi David I. Golovensky presided, and his wife, Muriel, and a friend, Nathan Cohen, served as witnesses.

From what I was told, Mom borrowed the wedding dress. She was never one of those women who dreamed of her wedding day. Broadway, yes; a wedding, no. For her, marriage was a means to get out of the house and be an adult.

—*Mallory*

I never saw them in love. I think he may have been. They used to have chicken fights—they would throw chicken across the table.

—*Lan O'Kun*

4. Her birth name was so far in her past that the bride first wrote "Shari" on her marriage registration certificate, then crossed it out and wrote "Phyllis N. Hurwitz."

The young couple—he was twenty-three and she had just turned twenty—moved into an apartment at Ninety-Sixth Street and Riverside Drive in Manhattan and worked full time on furthering their separate careers. Was the marriage utilitarian? Was Shari desperate to get out of the house? Perhaps both.

Lamb Chop literally came out of nowhere. Not right away, but eventually. Unraveling the legend isn't easy; half a century of myths have been knitted around the captivating sock puppet with whom Shari formed an iconic relationship that her daughter, Mallory, continues. It starts with the chance reunion of Shari with Mr. O'Kun's kid in a partnership that would flourish—despite some rocky moments—for forty years.

"I met him when I was eleven or twelve and he was the most brilliant pianist anybody had ever heard in our neighborhood," Shari said of Lan O'Kun. "Then I went to Music & Art and he went to Syracuse, and I started doing my own show and dancing and he was my first composer. Then he married my sister and now he writes our show as well."

"I was playing [piano] for all the [summer stock] dance auditions in the city of New York," says O'Kun. "They had them in March and April at various rooms around the country. One day I happened to be coming out of a room in Midtown Manhattan when Shari said, 'You're Mr. O'Kun's kid.' I said, 'Yeah.' She was auditioning. She said to me, 'What are you doing?' I said, 'I'm writing and I'm playing.' She says, 'Could you write me an act?' and I said, 'What do you do?' And she said, 'I'm a dancer and a magician. In fact, my father is a magician. In fact, he is the official magician for the City of New York.' She always said, 'knighted by LaGuardia.' I said, 'There's a perfect song. A song about your father teaching you magic and all the tricks'll go wrong.' She said, 'Could you write it?' I said, 'Instantly.' She said, 'By tomorrow morning?' 'Absolutely.' So I wrote it overnight. She was then living with her husband, Stan Lewis."

After her *Talent Scouts* victory, Shari made her featured debut on *Facts 'n' Fun* on July 5, 1953, on WRCA, the local NBC station. The origins of the booking differ; Shari liked to say that she and her husband Stan invented the show when she was laid up in bed with German measles (conflating rubella with the broken leg story) and her father handed her a ballpoint pen and said, "Write yourself a show." "He couldn't stand the fact that I was reading novels," she would say, "so I wrote a show and one of our uncles was a friend of Sid Caesar's manager, Leo Pillet. Leo took me directly to Steve Krantz,[5] who gave me an audition on camera and immediately bought the show." Other sources say the show had already been created and was owned by WRCA when Shari was hired to host it.[6]

"I met Shari when I was program director of the television station in New York owned by NBC," Krantz says. "I had a spot to fill on Sunday for a children's show, and Shari came in to see me. She was recommended by the manager of Sid Caesar, whom I knew, and she sat in my office and I was enchanted. She was magical and I was impressed by her. In that meeting I was the puppet because I fell in love with her. She did something, I don't remember exactly what, but if you talk about perky and pert and pretty and smart, she had all of those things going for her. She gave me a sample of what she could do, and then I set up an audition for her at the studio we had at 106th Street in New York."[7]

Steve Krantz was the husband of author Judy Krantz (the former Judy Tarcher, older sister of Shari's future husband Jeremy Tarcher). But Dad and Mom hadn't even met yet, so it was just happenstance and coincidence.

—*Mallory*

"You find somebody who gets you in, and then you're on your own," Shari said. "I was never brought up to identify with rejection. If I was getting rejection I would reevaluate myself. The ultimate luck for anybody is to be born into the right family at the right time and in the right city. Well, in New York City a lot of the people we knew were involved in

5. Within ten years of their first meeting, Steve Krantz would become Shari's brother-in-law when he married Judith Tarcher, the sister of Jeremy Tarcher (whom Shari married in 1958). As Judith Krantz, she became the best-selling author of *Scruples, Lovers,* and other novels.

6. DreamWorks Wiki, https://dreamworks.fandom.com/wiki/DreamWorks_Wiki.

7. Steve Krantz, interviewed in 1994.

> Children's programming in 1953 was a phenomenon that every television station in America believed in. They did it locally. There were things like *Ding Dong School* and *Romper Room* and other children's shows that were locally produced. It doesn't exist anymore. What you have is a great, massive input of children's programming produced either in New York or in Hollywood. These were the days before the Children's Television Workshop. The children's programming that was on the air, that I put on the air, were these tired old cartoons that were the remnants of Republic Pictures and . . . [Max and Dave Fleischer's] Out of the Inkwell, old Popeyes, things of that sort. It was before the days that producers were producing animation for television.
>
> —*Steve Krantz*

show business. My uncle wrote the photography column for the Associated Press and he put me together with Leo." And Leo Pillet led to Steve Krantz.

Krantz gave the show a thirteen-week pledge and reflected (at the time of his 1994 interview), "Shari has always had a deep commitment, not only to entertain but also to teach. She comes by it naturally. She has a deep, instinctive sense that not only should children's entertainment be entertaining, but there should be some values that come out of it. So the title *Facts 'n' Fun* really was the combination of elements that Shari is all about."

Although Shari always denied that Stan had any part in her career, Lan O'Kun vouches otherwise. "Stan Lewis gathered five of his sponsors and decided to do a show for his wife. I was the writer of that show. Not the only writer. There was a man who wrote *I Love a Mystery* [Carlton E. Morse] who started writing the show, and I was [also] writing the show—for $38. After a while, a very short while, five or six weeks, Shari fired him and I became *the* writer of the show."

In 1956 the Shari-Stan marriage ended. To this day, no one in the family agrees what happened or who pulled the plug. By the age of twenty-three, Shari Lewis had no husband. But she did have a new name. For the rest of her life she refused to discuss her first marriage; she would only say that it happened and that Stan died of a heart attack after they divorced.

Another bizarre coincidence: My college boyfriend's best friend was Stan Lewis's son from his second marriage. It was weird meeting what could have been my brother. I think there were like five Jews in New York at the time, and they all knew each other.

—*Mallory*

4

Shari Had a Little Lamb

Facts 'n' Fun (1953) combined Shari's love of magic and her desire to educate. The only problem was that the kids on the show didn't appreciate it. "Now here's something that only I could tell you," Lan O'Kun confides. "It was a segmentized show, a magazine show. One of the spots was where children appeared. She sat in the middle with Taffy Twinkle and I wrote funny questions for her to ask the kids. She'd say, 'And what do you think?' and the kid would jump a hundred feet." This is something O'Kun discloses with some difficulty: "The fact is that Shari is terrible with kids."

> Lanny wrote and Mom rewrote or tweaked. She had a hand in everything. However, no one ever has or ever will write as well for the puppets as my uncle Lanny—ever. Music, comedy—he's the king.
>
> —*Mallory*

Steve Krantz confirms, "She was using two wooden puppets: Taffy Twinkle and one called Samson. It wasn't until later on, a year or two later, that she invented Lamb Chop and Charlie Horse."

Even with her show gone, Shari was not out. She mailed a photo of herself (wearing her prom gown) and a female puppet to New York television station WPIX, asking for a job. "The gown was my prom gown from high school," she told WPIX's archive interviewer. "I went to Music and Art High School here in New York and I got out at 15 and that was my only professional picture. I had taken my dummy and put it on my knee and so that got me one of my first shows."[1]

1. WPIX Archive Facebook page (undated).

She got better with kids, but only a bit. She was a professional and hated working with non-pros. I'm pretty sure she actually didn't like sharing the spotlight with anyone. Hence: puppets. Kids are an X factor; you never know what you're going to get out of 'em. If you have ten kids onstage, you're gonna get a couple who'll be boring, a couple who'll be obnoxious, and probably one that is your gem. Shari didn't like an X factor onstage. This was her show and she was performing it for you to enjoy, whereas when I perform, we're all doing the show together. She was an old-school performer. It's a very generational thing. She would give you a brilliant show and expect you to thank her for it.

—*Mallory*

Facts 'n' Fun ended on September 26, 1953, in a manner typical for the television industry: Mom found out her show was canceled in an elevator leaving the studio for the day. She was small and was blocked by two big men. Another couple of guys got in the elevator and started talking about the cancellation, not knowing she was right there.

—*Mallory*

In 1955 she transitioned to New York's WPIX-TV, replacing Ted Steele as the host of *Kartoon Klub*. Two new puppets, Samson and Randy Rocket, accompanied Taffy Twinkle. "My shows are aimed at children from four to ten," she told *TV Guide* at the time. "These are the years when a child learns the difference between the real and the unreal." Airing weekdays, the show featured a live studio audience of children who watched as the host introduced cartoons, among them *Crusader Rabbit,* one of the first animated titles produced expressly for TV. On September 23, 1956, *Kartoon Klub* was renamed *Shari & Her Friends;* within the same year she was simultaneously doing a Saturday kids' show called *Shariland* and, in 1957, added the daily *Hi, Mom.* It was a grueling schedule. She also appeared on WABC-TV's *Look to Win* and continued to make guest appearances on Pinky Lee's NBC show, DuMont's *Wonderama,* and ABC's *Tinker's Toy Show.*

"New York was a glorious place in the fifties," says Mallory. "It was the era of *Mad Men* and Mom was the darling of New York." But it was still only local. Local television, even in New York, was important, but it wasn't the Big Time; it wasn't network, and it wasn't going out all over the country. On October 3, 1955, ABC had debuted Walt Disney's *Mickey Mouse Club,* an hour-long series that ran weekday afternoons and was aimed at primarily grammar school–aged children just returning home from classes. It remained for CBS to premiere, on October 30, 1955, a morning series devoted specifically to preschoolers: *Captain Kangaroo.*

Broadcast live from New York (unlike the *Mickey Mouse Club,* which was filmed in Los Angeles), *Captain Kangaroo* would become the most beloved and longest-running network children's program. Decidedly low-tech when it started, it featured Bob Keeshan as the alliterative officer, Hugh "Lumpy" Brannum as his neighbor Mr. Greenjeans, and other assorted characters including Grandfather Clock, Dancing Bear, Mr. Moose, and Bunny Rabbit, all of them manned by Cosmo Allegretti. Each weekday morning, young viewers were invited into the Treasure House for skits, songs, book readings, *Tom Terrific* cartoons, and lessons on how to grow up right. Such a puppet-friendly atmosphere begged for the presence of the young woman now known as Shari Lewis.

I had been discharged from the army and I turned on the television and there was Shari performing. I called her and said I'd decided to be a writer. We recalled our friendship and she said she didn't need a writer but she would be happy to have lunch and kibitz, and she introduced me to her then-writer Lan O'Kun, who was brilliant. I had lunch with him and out of gratitude I sent her a little script for the puppets. Well, she read that and called me and said, "I guess I do need a writer," and that's how it got started. I started writing for Shari in January of 1958.

—*Saul Turteltaub*

Shari always made Lamb Chop's origins sound magical, recalling on more than one occasion, "My father said, 'if Mary has a little lamb, why shouldn't Shari have a little lamb?'" She told the story countless times, but on one particular occasion she took special care to get it just right. For the A&E *Biography* series, she had agreed to be more frank than usual in discussing her life: "I was studying at that moment with Sandy Meisner of the Neighborhood Playhouse and I had learned how to do a basic Stanislavsky improvisation. So I took this lamb that I didn't know and sat in front of a mirror and I gave her something that she wanted from me. I gave myself an equally strong reason why she should not have it, which is what a Stanislavsky improvisation is all about. And we improvised. We finished. I got up and called Daddy and said, 'Hey Pop. You watch Saturday—this is it.' It was so clear that I had found myself *in* myself."[2]

Perhaps there was a purpose in keeping Lamb Chop's beginnings vague. "The story that I heard," recalls Mallory, "was that my grandfather had helped somebody in some way and the person came up to my grandfather and said, 'My daughter sews. I know your daughter does puppets. Do you think she'd want to use this?' and handed it to my grandfather, who said to [Shari], 'If Mary can have a little lamb, why can't Shari?' and she promptly threw it under the bed and did not take it out again until the *Captain Kangaroo* show called and said, 'We love you but we hate your dummies' because she was using big dummies, and she said, 'Uh, I have a lamb, his name is, uh, Lamb Chop.' Boom. That's the story I know."

> I was the junior [programming] executive in the department [at NBC] when I first met with Shari. I was a fan, but I was a fan of Lamb Chop's and Charlie Horse's. I took the meeting because I wanted to meet her. On top prime-time shows you may have been introduced to Shari Lewis, but she usually spoke through her characters. When the actual person walked into my office and sat down and talked to me, I was impressed by her wit, first of all, because she's very, very funny. Very quick-witted. But she was also very interesting, and she and I share a philosophy of children's television.
>
> —*Margaret Loesch*

Says Susan Miller, who handled the licensing of Lamb Chop and Shari's other properties from 1988 onward, "I recall her telling me that

2. This was the version Shari told in the A&E documentary.

she had hurt her leg or something and a cousin gave her a sock and she made it into a puppet and she taught herself ventriloquism when she was recovering. That's what I thought she told me."

Other origin stories are equally diverse and similarly enigmatic. The idea that Shari Lewis's career was built on an anonymous gift whose creator never attempted to collect on her largesse is significant. Indeed, Shari copyrighted Lamb Chop in her sole name as a "plastic doll" in 1957, a "soft sculpture" in 1960, and a "re-styling of doll and addition of plush material" in 1983. The latter registrations added Tarcher Productions as a coregistrant.[3]

Pressed for his knowledge of Lamb Chop's origins, Lan O'Kun reaches back. Shari "was invited by *Captain Kangaroo* to play a segment," he says. "She wondered what she should do on the show and she said that she just had these two puppets that had been made by, I think, a hat-maker in San Francisco. Who knows where she got them from? She had got them in a package and they were wonderful but she had never tried them. She put Lamb Chop on and I fell apart. It was the first time I thought 'talent.' It was magic. The first time you see Lamb Chop? Incredible. I was as blown away as everybody who has ever seen Lamb Chop. It was life, immediately, and I said, 'We'll put the big dummy aside and that's what we'll use.'" In other words, the only thing that almost everybody agrees on is that somebody else, some woman, created the Lamb Chop puppet. "Yes," affirms O'Kun. "I've never met her, never heard of her."

The mystery of Lamb Chop's DNA was solved when New York architect Carl Stein was sorting through the possessions of his late mother, Ethel Stein, who died at age one hundred in March 2018. He subsequently contacted Mallory to tell her what he had found. "My parents had lived in the same house since 1946 and had saved almost everything," he said. "My first reaction was to just clear it all out. I started but realized there was stuff that had to be gone through. It took me a year. Then, recently, I was with my dog at the dog run in Washington Square Park early one

3. Original registration number GU28846; http://cocatalog.loc.gov/cgi-bin/Pwebrecon.cgi?v1=21&ti=1,21&Search%5FArg=Lewis%2C%20Shari&Search%5FCode=NALL&CNT=25&PID=u8dKxJREZ7KNRBBjMEmxgK9pALd-&SEQ=20170409191947&SID=1.

morning. I was talking to a few of the regulars, and someone—one of the 'youngsters'—said that they had just seen an old tape of the ventriloquist Shari Lewis. I said, 'Oh, my mother made Lamb Chop.' They said, 'Oh my God!'" Stein immediately started digging through his mother's papers and found the connection that had eluded historians for decades.

Ethel Stein was a remarkable woman. Growing up in a family of artists, she earned a living designing and making theater sets and costumes. In her early career as an artist, however, she was a sculptor. She studied with Bauhaus cofounder Josef Albers and was influenced by the weaving of Albers's wife, Anni. Later, when Stein was in her forties and physical issues prevented her from sculpting, she rediscovered her early fascination with weaving. Eventually, she explored new forms of the craft, designing and building a sophisticated hand loom that is now part of the permanent collection of the Chicago Art Institute. More than forty of her weavings are housed there, as well as at the Metropolitan Museum, Cooper-Hewitt, and Cleveland Museum of Art. In 2016 a retrospective exhibition of her work at the Chicago Art Institute classified her as "master weaver."

Before becoming a master weaver, however, she was a puppet maker, and in 1956 she patented[4] a design for a sock puppet that was the progenitor of Lamb Chop. "My mother had been making these puppets primarily for various fund-raisers, and whether it was her idea or some friends' idea, she decided to go into production of sock puppets," Carl Stein says. "Puppets were a small part of her life's work but whatever she did, she did with incredible focus on detail and fine-grain information." Her merchandising foray, however, was a bust: a line of animals called Doodleheads cost more to produce than could be recouped by sales, and the company failed with ten thousand units on hand—or, rather, off hands. "And when she ended up with a lot of unsold stock," Carl says, "she hired someone to demonstrate them at what I think was Kresge's Five and Dime on Fifth Avenue. Shari Lewis saw them there and recognized the possibilities for her work."

Coincidentally, this was after Shari's successful first appearance on *Captain Kangaroo* and after the producers told her to get rid of the

4. US Patent Office, "Puppet Doll" #2,762,163, September 11, 1956.

wooden vent dummy if she wanted to come back. After seeing Stein's puppets, Shari sent a letter to the Doodlehead company. "It's an interesting letter," Carl says, "handwritten to 'Sir.' Then there are a couple of letters back and forth between lawyers about the rights. I don't remember what the final value, the final fee for Lamb Chop was, but it was remarkably small. I do know that there was some more discussion regarding the later puppets and that Shari Lewis bought the entire rights." Lamb Chop's direct predecessor was a rabbit puppet Ethel had designed and made for one of the fund-raisers. A visual comparison is stunning. "The detail on that rabbit was not that different from Lamb Chop," Carl says. "It's a different tone—Lamb Chop is a very sweet, perfect companion for Shari—I really don't know how their dialogue developed but, clearly, Shari Lewis's input was critical to the dynamics between the two of them and to Lamb Chop's development."

Ethel's story is an interesting one that deserves mention because it adds color to Shari's efforts to achieve success in an age when men ruled the business world. "As I was going through [my mother's] papers," Carl says, "I found that, despite her protestations to the contrary, she was remarkably well organized, lots of detail, very sort of systems oriented in terms of planning. She presented herself as a kind of dumb blond. One of her idols was Judy Holliday. She was completely on her own from the time she was sixteen and was working finding places to live. That's a story in itself. She had a lot of jobs, doing set design, set painting, costume design, and costume making. She worked at [the club] Café Society where Judy Holliday got her start. When I was a kid, she'd always tell me, 'Gotta look at *Bells Are Ringing* or *Adam's Rib.*' I think that was a model of the way my mother saw herself. Also, until she was about thirteen, Ethel was raised by her aunt and uncle. Abbo Ostrowsky (uncle) founded the art school at the Educational Alliance, whose students included Chaim Gross, the Sawyer brothers, and Zero Mostel, who, incidentally, was also a significant performer at Café Society. She was pretty much immersed in art from a very early age. I'm not sure how she got to Boston, but when she was nineteen she worked as a stage designer under the name 'Ethel Lynn' because Ethel Levy, which was her maiden name, couldn't get a job in Boston in those days. That said, she did have a strong sense of how things worked onstage, and that, along with the costume work, had a strong effect on her involvement with puppets. And all of this was integral to her becoming one of the best-known textile artists in the world. The creation of the puppets," Carl continues, "and I'm sort of piecing this together, and my perception of time back then is very different than it is now—but it seems to me that the puppets for Shari Lewis were made over about a year's period, so there must have been quite a bit of conversation during that time."

At some point, Ethel and Shari had a falling out over something, but there is no record of what it was. Perhaps the experience inspired Ethel Stein to take charge of her own business affairs and, like Shari, forge a name for herself as a leader in her field. Says Carl, "I don't know whether it's related to that, but later, with any sale of the pieces of art, my mother was clear about getting certain copyright provisions rolled in." As for Shari's craft, Carl says, "I've seen a few pieces of her work and the animation that she brought to those puppets is incredible. For whatever personal tensions may have existed, artistically it was a great success, a meeting of the minds."

Shari had had the original Lamb Chop since she was a teenager. This thing had never been cleaned. We called up Windsor Cleaners, a place in the Bronx that did a lot of theatrical costumes. This was a really emotional thing for Shari to give Lamb Chop over.

—*Mary Lou Brady*

Launder the puppets? Sure. I had a system for doing that. I figured out a method where I could literally throw Lamb Chop in the washing machine. I'd take the eyelashes off, the ears off, the tongue out, so that nothing faded on her, and I would literally wash it in the washing machine in my shop. The eyelashes were just glued on, so I'd peel them off. It was just Elmer's glue. She went in a [net] bag. Then I would take her out and let her air-dry. I tried putting one in the dryer in the spin cycle, and when I took her out she was about four feet long. It was frightening. I still have a picture of her inside the washing machine. I put it up in my shop with a sign that said, "Don't try this at home."

—*Pat Brymer*

When Carl contacted Mallory to set the record straight, Mallory was pleased to finally have Lamb Chop's lineage revealed. The parentage of one of Shari's other puppets is more precise. "Hush Puppy *I* did," says Lan O'Kun. "Hush Puppy I drew and had stuffed and I gave him to Shari as a Christmas present. And we had the gang."

There were, from time to time, other characters that came and went. There was a crow named Wing Ding who spouted beatnik argot ("yeah, man" and "cool"), but she quickly flew south or, more accurately, into O'Kun's home office, where she now roosts. Mimi Owl was an ersatz Zsa Zsa Gabor, and there was a rabbit named Hopscotch that quickly disappeared, perhaps because he was too similar to Captain Kangaroo's beloved Bunny Rabbit. The original Lamb Chop has seen better days—sixty years of them—and is contentedly resting in a comfortable closet dwelling in Mallory's home.

Lamb Chop has remained a star for more than six decades. Over the years she has stayed the same precocious six-year-old she was when she was born—er, knitted. The big question has always been whether she is Shari's alter ego. "We always thought of Lamb Chop as being Shari as

---

If Lamb Chop is such a cultural icon, she ought to be in the Smithsonian along with the ruby slippers from *The Wizard of Oz* and Jimmy Olsen's bow tie from *The Adventures of Superman*. But she isn't.

She had that opportunity back in 1980. There was a huge puppet exhibit at the Smithsonian: Charlie McCarthy, Kermit the Frog, all the popular puppets of that era were there—except Lamb Chop. Shari never wanted to see Lamb Chop inanimate, sitting on a pole. That's why it never got to a museum. She didn't want any of her puppets to be seen unless they were on her hand.

—*Pat Brymer*

The Smithsonian has approached me a number of times about acquiring Lamb Chop. The only Lamb Chop that's on exhibit is in David Copperfield's museum. He's been a friend of the family for decades.

—*Mallory*

---

she would like to have been as a child," says O'Kun. Adds Pat Brymer, Shari's master puppeteer and the person who made Lamb Chop and all her clothing for the last forty years of Shari's life, "Lamb Chop is a person. Lamb Chop sits there and she has discussions with you, and you can talk to Lamb Chop about anything, and she always has a response. There's no problem with that."

"Lamb Chop is a princess," says Bernie Rothman, who was Shari's coproducer on later shows. "She wants to go to the mall and shop and she wants to be a bit of a brat sometimes. I don't mean this literally, but I'm saying all the things that Shari probably wanted to be when she was a little girl but was much too responsible to be."[5] Steve Krantz agrees: "I think Lamb Chop is the naughty side of Shari Lewis, and there is such a side." He wouldn't elaborate.

"Lamb Chop is real," insists Gary H. Grossman, and he's only half joking. "I've talked to Lamb Chop. I've met Lamb Chop. And Shari, although she practiced routines, said that 'if I have to think about what Lamb Chop is going to say, I might as well not say it,' and I believed that. I worked one-on-one with Shari [Grossman was also a producer on *Entertainment Tonight*]. You'd have to ask Lamb Chop direct questions, and it was like Lamb Chop answering as Lamb Chop would, totally unscripted. That came from [Shari's] genius, because everything else she did was rehearsed." Plus, when they're interviewed side by side, Grossman notes, Lamb Chop gets her own lapel mike to seal the illusion.

> Barbara [Shari's younger sister] is the essence of Lamb Chop. Lamb Chop was always a sibling, a hurt kid. Think about this. When Shari started with Lamb Chop, how old was Barbara? She's nine years younger. Think about Lamb Chop's attitude and strange way of getting at a point and asking it innocently. Shari was taking Barbara and putting that essence into the puppet. Lanny [O'Kun] has told me this several times, but he doesn't know it. Where did Shari get that character? It's Barbara.
>
> —*Brad Hood*

5. Bernard Rothman, interviewed in 1994.

When it comes to armchair psychology and analyzing her relationship with her characters, Shari puts a sock in it. "I don't articulate feelings through the puppets," she states unequivocally. "I mean, certainly when I'm in a sketch doing comedy or drama with the puppets, I trust them. But we're not ad-libbing—although I don't always write everything for Lamb Chop. Sometimes when I'm finishing an interview, say for Larry King, I'll come off and I won't remember what I have said. I'll remember what *I* have said, but I'll phase out what *she* said. She's trustworthy."

> I once was doing Lamb Chop at a Telemundo event and she was sitting on some man's shoulder talking rapidly in Spanish. I barely speak Spanish and I remember thinking, "I wonder what she is saying?" She also can hit notes an octave higher than I can. It doesn't make sense, but I don't question it.
>
> —*Mallory*

Shari made it back onto *Captain Kangaroo* on March 2, 1957. She remembered the day not only because it brought her to the Treasure House but also because that night she had her first date with her future husband, Jeremy Tarcher.

5

A Show of Her Own

There's something that needs to be noted at this point: Shari Lewis broke the mold right from the start just by being who she was: a female ventriloquist.

"There was no other woman before her at that level with that range," says Lisa Sweazy, curator of the Vent Haven Museum in Fort Mitchell, Kentucky. Opened in 1973 by W. S. Berger, a lifelong fan of the art, the museum is a repository of ventriloquial lore, including Berger's encouraging correspondence with a very young Shari. "There were other female ventriloquists, but Shari was in a class by herself," Sweazy notes. "A lot of women felt either compelled to do a slightly sexualized act, almost a burlesque element, dressed in seductive outfits—not strip-tease, but a more showy performance. Or there were many examples where a woman in her thirties dressed in pigtails like her dummy and was juvenile. Shari was neither of those. She took the 'boys club' to task and was accepted as exactly who she was."

She was also beginning to specialize in what people who didn't know any better called a "dying art" that demanded "reinvention." "The minute I got into ventriloquism," recalls Jay Johnson, who, along with his puppet "Bob," starred in the 1977–1981 TV series *Soap,* "somebody said, 'it's a dying art, I don't know what you're gonna do,' but, for a dying art, I sure stay busy. When I left *Soap* I figured it was just a matter of time before ABC called me with a production deal, so I wrote a lot of shows to star myself and I pitched a lot of things and everybody liked it but eventually—I had always performed in clubs—and comedy clubs started being very much in vogue, and the big corporates before 2007 were just a candy machine. Everybody was having big fun, big money. *Reinvent* is more of an intellectual term. I think we all reinvent ourselves cuz we got another job. You just do what you can."

It was a combination of novelty and skill that got Shari onto *Captain Kangaroo,* but she still needed to expand her appeal. From 1957 to 1959 she headlined the series *Hi, Mom* and added two more cuddly creations, each with distinct personalities: Charlie Horse and Hush Puppy.

At the same time, she began a Saturday series called *Shariland.* Even for a workaholic, the regimen was challenging. "She had two shows on," says Saul Turteltaub, whose luncheon pitch had landed him a job writing for her. "She had a local show on daily called *Hi, Mom* which was one of those morning shows where Josie McCarthy told people how to eat and Nurse Jane [told] people how to get better after they ate what Josie McCarthy made, and Shari with guests. Then on Saturday we had *Shariland* which was a show for the kids. Lan and I wrote all six shows for which I got sixty dollars a week. I think he got three hundred. He deserved my sixty. That's how it started."[1]

Doing two shows at the same time set the mad pace that Shari and Lan—then in their twenties—dared themselves to maintain. "The two of us did six hours of television a week *ourselves,*" says O'Kun, still amazed.

"And it was really tough," adds Shari, "because I'm very nearsighted, a little bit cockeyed, I mean I can't see anything, and so I had to memorize ten, twelve songs a week, thirty-six pages of script a week, twelve commercials a day, and do that for six days a week."

"She'd run on the air and do the show," O'Kun continues, "get off the air, we'd talk about the next day, she'd go home, begin memorizing songs, I would write the next day, and so it would go over and over again."

It was grueling, but it was TV. "You really have no time to do any prep," Shari said. "You get filled in, and then you go on, and you shoot from the hip."

Shariland debuted October 13, 1956, and *Hi, Mom* debuted August 14, 1957. What made them do-able was the variety created by Shari's three well-defined puppet characters: Lamb Chop, Hush Puppy, and Charlie Horse. Each had its purpose in dramatic situations. "Different things

1. Saul Turteltaub, interviewed by Adrienne Faillace, May 12, 2016, for Television Academy.com.

come out through each of them," Shari said of the popular trio. "Lamb Chop is the most vulnerable of the three and the most impish. Charlie Horse is the brash, aggressive side of me." Adds Mallory, "Charlie Horse's acerbic personality was certainly based on Lan." Both women agree that Hush Puppy is the one who is confused, but he is also the peacemaker—probably the sweetest. Although there have been other puppets over the years, it took *Hi, Mom* to make Lamb Chop, Charlie Horse, and Hush Puppy an enduring and endearing troika.

"Hush Puppy is a real middle child,"[2] Shari says. "He makes peace between the older and the younger. He is less secure than the others. Plays by himself. Lamb Chop is a classic third child, spoiled, indulgent. Charlie Horse is very much like me. I have to watch myself with Charlie Horse because he wants what he wants and he is very self-centered and self-focused."

"Hush Puppy's logic is wonderful," adds Mallory. "He's not very bright, but somehow he sees the truth where the other smarter siblings often miss it. And Lamb Chop just stomps her little foot and wants what she wants and she's the baby and used to being indulged. I'm an only child so I guess I'm a combination of all three."

Television was the perfect close-up way for Shari to get into people's lives. For an entertainer who wanted to reach children or families, the best way was a single-shot or a two-shot. That was what worked best for Buffalo Bob and Howdy Doody—watching the puppets on a puppet stage. It's what worked for Captain Kangaroo so well. But for Shari it was a close-up medium, and then a bond. Captain Kangaroo seemed to be talking to people all the time, and Howdy Doody was presenting stories. Shari was just having a conversation with Lamb Chop, and we were eavesdropping. So television was just perfect for her. Either television was invented for Shari or Shari was invented for television.

—*Gary H. Grossman*

---

2. "Middle child" is the description Shari developed to disguise the slow-talking Hush Puppy's original concept as a southern hick.

I had enormous respect for what she did. The energy that radiated from her was absolutely nonstop. I'm not sure she made the distinction between being a children's entertainer and being an entertainer for everybody. She just did what she did. She didn't want to be constrained in one area. She wanted to do what she did as well as she could do it and keep working at it, and wherever it took her, it took her.

—*Sonny Fox*

"It would be easy to identify Lamb Chop, Charlie Horse, and Hush Puppy as simple, subpersonalities of Shari's," Jeremy Tarcher parses carefully, "but they are, in fact, constructed personalities."

When he and Shari met, Jeremy held what he described as a "totally minor" job at a competing television station—WNEW-TV—where he had risen from the mail room to become the public service director. One day in 1957 he paid a visit to a friend who was performing on one of Shari's shows. He saw her and was smitten. "I think I felt myself a little bit outclassed," he says, and immediately forgot about his friend. "I invited her out for a drink and thought, well, if the drink goes well, I'll invite her out for dinner. At the end of the first drink I said, 'Let's go out to dinner,' and at that point I learned something about Shari. She does not leave time open. Because she said, 'I have a dinner date.' And I thought to myself, 'Oh dear, I certainly have planned this badly.' So I said, 'I'd like to come with you,' and, astonishingly, she said, 'Fine.'" It is not recorded how Shari's original dinner date felt about the interloper.

Doc and Ann Hurwitz, however, were a different matter, and kid sister Barbara intervened to ensure that things went well. "Shari was dating Jeremy," Barbara says, "and my parents wanted to meet him. Shari kept procrastinating. We lived in the Bronx. She never brought Jeremy home. Finally she said, 'Okay,' and she sent him by train [without her]. I was thirteen and I thought, 'Oh, this poor guy. He's gonna come and meet my parents and she isn't even with him?' I walked a mile to go to the train station. I see this nice-looking young man come down the stairs and I think, 'He's very good looking. Good.' We started to walk and I said, 'Jeremy, what do you do?' and he said, 'Why do I have to do anything?' I said, 'You mean, you don't do *anything*?' and he said, 'No; why do I *have* to do anything?' I stopped him on the street—we [later] laughed about this—and I grabbed him by the collar and I said, 'You have one mile to decide what you do before you meet my parents because that's the first question they're going to ask you.' He came from a relatively wealthy family and he was not at all ambitious. Shari was very ambitious and she motivated him. But he was very smart and he created a whole niche and developed a very successful company. It isn't like he didn't know what he was doing."

Ultimately, Jeremy became a publisher—Tarcher Press—which specialized in New Age and self-help books. It is now part of Penguin USA.

Jeremy Phillip Tarcher (born January 2, 1922) grew up with advantages. His father headed an advertising agency, and his mother was a lawyer. Although the family was well read, Jeremy admitted that he was the exception—an irony, given his eventual success as a publisher. He had a hard time getting into college but was accepted by St. John's in Annapolis, Maryland—also an irony, given that St. John's was celebrated for its "Great Books" curriculum.

"Jeremy was a great publisher," Barbara continues, "a lazy guy but a very talented publisher. He needed a lot of self-help, so he looked into the self-help area. It's not an area Shari shared *at all.* I asked him what he would do when Shari died and he said, 'I'll write the book Shari wouldn't let me write,' and I said, 'What was that?' and he said, 'A book about drugs.' But by [the time she died] there was no market for the book."

Dad was very handsome when he was younger and he was from a fancy Jewish family, and that mattered. Mom married up, although the truth of the matter was that Dad was making fifty bucks a week while Mom was making five thousand bucks a week or whatever it was, and my aunt Judy [Krantz] told my father not to marry my mother because he would never be as successful as she was. My father, being an idiot, told my mother that Judy said that, and Judy and Steve were not invited to their wedding.

—*Mallory*

On March 15, 1958, Jeremy and Shari were married. Technically, this made her Phyllis Naomi Tarcher, but she kept the professional name Shari Lewis.

Shari at last achieved major network status on October 1, 1960, with *The Shari Lewis Show*. It ran for three years on NBC (until September 28, 1963), and that is how most people of a certain generation became aware of her. This is partly because she reached a national audience but also because the production values were such that Shari, Lan, the musicians, and various guest stars could stretch their abilities for half an hour every Saturday morning—in color.

> There were three channels in those days. Three. And most people had only one TV in the house. One. So if the TV was on, there was a one in three chance they were watching Mom, and by "they" I mean the whole family.
>
> —*Mallory*

Of historical significance—primarily to Shari and those who follow children's television—is the fact that *The Shari Lewis Show* pushed *Howdy Doody* off the air. Created in 1947 by E. Roger Muir, Howdy Doody was a marionette—a freckle-faced, red-haired boy in cowboy garb—voiced by former announcer "Buffalo" Bob Smith (né Robert Schmidt) of Buffalo, New York, who also hosted the show. Howdy was manipulated by Frank Paris for the first year; he then departed over an intellectual property dispute, and a new Doody was crafted by someone working for Disney (decades before such artists were called "imagineers"). For thirteen years, *Howdy Doody* held sway over America's children, welcoming them each weekday at 4:30 with the question, "Say, kids, what time is it?" and cueing the delighted (and well-rehearsed) response from the Peanut Gallery, "It's Howdy Doody time!" Everybody would then launch into the theme song, sung to the tune of "Ta-Ra-Ra-Boom-De-Ay."

Howdy's regular marionette cohorts were the fulminating Mayor Phineas T. Bluster, the wholesome Dilly Dally, the indefinable Flub-a-Dub, and John J. Fadoozle, the world's number one (*boing*) pa-rivate eye.

Live characters included Chief Thunderthud, Princess Summerfallwinterspring, and Clarabell the Clown, originally played by Bob Keeshan, who left over a salary dispute in 1952 and resurfaced at rival CBS three years later as Captain Kangaroo.

Howdy Doody was one of the first kiddie shows to both entrance and exploit children. They tuned in religiously every day to see the latest exploits of Howdy, Bob, and the denizens of Doodyville. In the days before the FCC forbade onscreen hosts to hawk goods, Howdy and Buffalo Bob pushed Wonder Bread, Three Musketeers candy bars, Paul Parrot shoes, and Hostess Twinkies, Creme-filled Cupcakes, and Snowballs. While all this was going out over the air, the kids in the studio took part in western games and sing-alongs.

Howdy Doody's last broadcast was in NBC Living Color™ on September 24, 1960. It was a tearful departure as Bob packed up the relics of Doodyville, everybody said good-bye, and even the normally silent Clarabell talked.

There wasn't any public blowback against Shari for replacing *Howdy Doody*. Howdy's fans had grown up and left Doodyville, and it was simply television attrition. In fact, laying off half a dozen performers, many of whom had been giving management a hard time, might have been attractive to the network higher-ups.

Still, Shari never forgot what had happened to Buffalo Bob and realized that it could happen to her if she didn't stay ahead of the game. She decided then and there that she was going to be in charge of herself, her career, and her show. In an age when many still thought that women belonged in the kitchen, Shari was going to make the industry bend in her direction, and she would bring the children with her.

"I've never thought being dumb was a good thing," she said, articulating her philosophy. "Somebody asked me what my goal is with kids and I said, 'to lead them where I'm going.' They said, 'Where are you going?' I said, 'I'm going to a place where it's cool to be smart and it's smart to be classy and where it's classy to be a doer rather than a viewer.' It's stupid to try to be ordinary and dull." And to the end of her days, she never was.

6

Rising Stars

The Shari Lewis Show proved the perfect showcase for the twenty-seven-year-old. Airing at 10:00 a.m. Eastern time on Saturdays (*Howdy Doody*'s old slot), its 137 episodes from October 1, 1960, to September 28, 1963, were essentially miniature musical comedies or, in theater parlance, "book shows." They were written by Saul Turteltaub, Mickey Rose, and Lan O'Kun, with O'Kun composing the songs. It was also the first children's show produced in color. (At the time, NBC, which was owned by RCA, was trying to get the public to drop $400 for color sets—a huge expense in an era when the minimum wage was $1 an hour.)

The production schedule developed by Shari and her team was based on NBC's irrevocable order that the show would be taped from exactly 6:00 to 6:30 p.m. on Thursday in Studio 3K of the network's facility at 30 Rockefeller Center. This meant that rehearsals would be held Monday, Tuesday, and Wednesday at Dance Players Studio at Sixth Avenue and 49th Street, across from NBC. Thursday afternoon would be devoted to camera blocking, and at 6:00 sharp the engineers would start to roll tape. The programs were recorded live to tape, straight through, with no retakes. On Friday, key staff would meet at the Tarchers' apartment at 980 Riverside Drive to start preparing the next show.

Typical of the way Shari collected people is how Mary Lou Brady became her assistant in the fall of 1961. Hired as a temp while the show's regular production secretary was on vacation, Brady had previously worked for publicist Arthur P. Jacobs,[1] and she had a ball assisting Shari, whom she met for the first time at the rehearsal hall. "I had this enormous

1. Jacobs handled Shari's publicity. He later became a producer and made *Planet of the Apes* and *Doctor Dolittle*.

desk and my office was a locker," she says. "No kidding. I would come in in the morning, unlock it, and take out my typewriter and the files, and that was my office. I'd come home at night and tell my husband (who was a musician with the Les Elgart Band), 'Oh I really like this.' After the two weeks was up, that was it. Two or three weeks later I get a call from Jeremy saying, 'We were really happy when you were here,' that whatever-her-name-was had left, and did I want the job? I was thrilled. I go into my office—which is the locker—and what I heard from [associate producer] Frank Lewis and a couple of the other people was that, apparently, when [the other secretary] came back the crew were saying how much they had liked 'the girl who had replaced her.' Her nose got out of joint and she gave two weeks' notice. Whether that's true or not I don't know, but I like the story because it makes me look good. My first title was P.A. (production assistant), then they promoted me to assistant to the producer. It was the same job, just another title." Six decades later, "May-Oo," as Mallory called her, is still a dear family friend.

In addition to the highly skilled NBC technical crew, *The Shari Lewis Show* was produced (including booth directing) primarily by Robert Scheerer, with guest producers Jed Horner, Robert Hultgren, and Larry Blyden, among others.[2] Make no mistake, though; the real director was Shari Lewis.

The set was constructed around her size, movements, and abilities. It consisted of a fence, a house, and a yard used for dance sequences, all of them surrounding a performance area. The studio space was so small that nothing could be moved or extended, or they would have been broadcasting from the hallway. Episodes were shot with a standard three-camera setup, and overhead mikes on booms picked up the dialogue. This inevitably led to the classic ventriloquism audio blooper.

"We had the same crew all the time," Brady relates, "but one time Red McKinnon, our boom guy, was on vacation and we brought in a replacement and we're all up in the control room and we can't hear Lamb Chop. We can't figure out what's wrong. Finally Bobby Scheerer goes downstairs to look. We're up in the control room wondering what the

2. Blyden later gained renown as a Broadway actor (*The Apple Tree, Absurd Person Singular*) and chat show personality.

hell's going on. The boom man was so enchanted that he was moving the mike away from Shari and over Lamb Chop."

The placement of the puppets was worked out to the point of ritual. Lamb Chop was always on Shari's right hand with her elbow pointing upstage so that the left side of her face was always toward camera. (According to showbiz superstition, the left side of the face looks better in right-handed people, and the right side of the face looks better in left-handed people; beyond that, Shari was simply right-handed.) Other puppets such as Charlie Horse and Hush Puppy could sit on either hand. The fence was constructed with a ledge on which Shari rested her elbow to position Lamb Chop at the proper camera height. "If she had to change puppets," Brady says, "Frank Lewis would be behind the fence on his knees and he would pull off one puppet out of camera range and put another one on."

The series was a boon not only for Shari and her puppets but also for its guest stars. It gave Shari the opportunity to introduce her young viewers to performers she and her collaborators knew personally or admired, and she could now offer them airtime and a paycheck. British actor Ronald Radd played a continuing character called Mr. Goodfellow. Burr Tillstrom, creator of the Kuklapolitans (Kukla, Fran, and Ollie), appeared beginning on December 3, 1960, albeit without future human partner Fran Allison. Up-and-coming comic actor Morty Gunty was the guest on November 4, 1961. David Burns, then costarring in the Broadway hit *A Funny Thing Happened on the Way to the Forum,* appeared on February 9, 1963. Agnes Moorehead, who began as one of Orson Welles's Mercury Players, visited Shari's ensemble on June 29, 1963. One of the most frequent guests was Margaret Hamilton, popularly known as the Wicked Witch of the West from *The Wizard of Oz.* On four occasions

---

I met Margaret Hamilton when I was five. She was sitting in the living room at our Beverly Hills house when I came home from school. I took one look at her and *clearly* saw the Wicked Witch, and I burst into tears and ran screaming up the stairs to my room. My mom was *horrified*, but Margaret assured her, "This happens all the time." Poor lady!

—*Mallory*

---

she played Lamb Chop's gentle babysitter: February 16 and 23 and April 13 and 27, 1963.

Fred Gwynne, then known for *Car 54, Where Are You?* (on which Shari guest-starred February 4, 1962, and April 7, 1963)—years before he became Herman Munster—played Lamb Chop's doctor on whom the woolly puppet developed a crush. In addition to being an actor and a dancer, Gwynne wrote and illustrated children's books. He later played the memorable Judge Chamberlain Haller in the 1992 movie *My Cousin Vinny*. "Barbara and I saw him on Broadway in a show,"[3] Lan O'Kun enthuses. "He was tall and had long legs and that long face and he was just funny. He became part of a poker group that played at our house every Sunday. He was a quick study and a bright man who played guitar, could sculpt—you name it. Fred could do anything except play poker. But he could make you laugh at the table read."

Jerry Orbach, at the start of a remarkable stage and TV career, first appeared with Shari on May 26, 1962. He would be on the show another eleven times. "Jerry Orbach was playing a puppeteer on Broadway in *Carnival!* about a circus on the streets of France (adapted for the stage from the 1953 film *Lili*)," says O'Kun. Puppeteer Tom Tichenor created and operated the musical's remarkable puppets. "I thought it would be funny," O'Kun continues, "to have the puppets he was playing in his show appear with Lamb Chop and Charlie Horse. He was a delightful man and you could have a good conversation with him."

It was the Kennedy years, and for one sketch the show needed someone to do a JFK impression on a phone call. The man they picked was a young actor just starting out by the name of Alan Alda. "At the time he was just known as Robert Alda's son,"[4] says Brady, whose job included booking guests requested by Shari, her writers, and the producers.

Ossie Davis, then starring on Broadway in his play *Purlie Victorious*, appeared on May 5, 1962. Davis, a TV newcomer, became the only performer who literally stopped the show. "In all the years the only person

3. Probably *Irma La Douce*, in which Gwynne played Polyte-le-Mou.

4. A well-known film actor (*Rhapsody in Blue, The Man I Love*), Robert Alda played Sky Masterson in the original Broadway cast of *Guys and Dolls*. Alan, of course, became an American institution on television's *M*A*S*H*.

who screwed up and required a redo was Ossie Davis," Brady says. "Isn't that shocking? I'm not sure he understood that [we recorded live to tape]. It was so surprising; it wasn't exactly Hamlet's soliloquy that we were doing."

The person who scored the biggest hit was Dom DeLuise. A fellow Music & Art graduate, DeLuise made his first-ever television appearance on May 19, 1962, playing the "ineffective detective" Kenny Ketchum. Lamb Chop talked him into posing as her and getting into a baby carriage while Margaret Hamilton was babysitting. "Here I was, 18 years old and working with the great Shari Lewis and Lamb Chop," DeLuise wrote in his 1997 cookbook/memoir *Eat This Too.* "I was thrilled out of my mind because I was not only working with Shari but I also had a scene with the Wicked Witch of the [West] from *The Wizard of Oz,* Margaret Hamilton. As mean and as green as she was in the movie, she is as gentle and sweet . . . in real life."[5] Hamilton invited the young DeLuise to her home for tea. "Miss Hamilton and I talked about Mae West and W. C. Fields and I was in heaven," he wrote. He returned to Shari's show on February 23, 1963.

DeLuise remained a favorite of Shari's, who cast him thirty years later as Cookie the Chef in *The Charlie Horse Music Pizza,* and he became an even closer friend of Lan and Barbara O'Kun. He was, in a sense, Lan O'Kun's discovery; he was appearing in a show called *The Taboo Review* when O'Kun saw him, deemed him "the funniest man alive," and made a mental note. At the time, DeLuise was in New York on hiatus from the Cleveland Playhouse. When he returned to New York to appear in an adaptation of a Molière comedy, the two men reconnected, and Lan invited him to appear on Shari's show. "He was always funny," O'Kun reports, "but it was difficult writing for Dom because he liked to ad-lib."

Brady readily agrees. "Among the most wonderful experiences was the first time Dom DeLuise came to do the show. He was fun from that moment and became a regular. When Dom did the first read-through, I was in the other room and it was the first time I heard screams of laughter on a first reading. Not only was he wonderfully talented, he was a sweet, funny, dear man. He came to dinner at our apartment a few times. I met

5. Dom DeLuise, *Eat This Too: It'll Also Make You Feel Better* (New York: Pocket Books, 1997).

Carol [Arthur, the Broadway actress] when they were going together. It was a wonderful time." DeLuise and Arthur later married and had three sons, Peter, Michael, and David, all of whom went into show business.

New York had its share of top musicians, and Shari and Lan attracted some of the best. The show's three staff musical talents were Eddie Safranski (bass), Tony Gattuso (guitar), and Howie Breuer (drums). O'Kun, of course, was on piano and was responsible for most of the music and songs. He was prolific and fast, which meant that his lead sheets (basic written music) were sometimes jotted in haste. For this reason, improvising on themes was not only permitted; it was necessary. "These three NBC staff musicians could look at his chicken scratches and make music out of them," said Brady. "This was a problem for him because, after the show went off the air, [Lan] became music director for Jimmy Dean, and Peter Matz was the conductor. From what I hear there was trouble because Peter Matz would get these chicken scratches and say, 'What the fuck is *this*?'"

Shari's ventriloquial craft was impeccable and unique. The most difficult words for a ventriloquist to pronounce are those containing the labial consonants *B, F, M, P,* and *V.* Ventriloquists have devised various techniques to avoid them, from using glottal approximations such as *G* instead of *B* or *N* instead of *M* to shaking their dummy as a distraction.[6] Shari didn't need such tricks; remarkably, she spoke the labials as easily as any other sound. Mallory has the same facility.

Lamb Chop was also unique. Unlike traditional vent dummies, she can actually articulate words. "When the mouth moves," notes Brady, "it moves in the way that the word is formed. Think about that. On a lot of other puppets the mouth just goes up and down, where, with Lamb Chop, the mouth goes the way people speak." Shari learned to move her thumb and fingers inside the puppet's mouth to approximate the movement of lips.

"Shari would try to work something out just to see how it looked," Brady reports. "She would sit in the middle of the bed in the apartment with her script around her, she'd have the puppets, and that's how she

6. Some, like Edgar Bergen, never even bothered. Next time you see one of his performances, take your eyes off Charlie McCarthy and watch him.

A handful of ventriloquists are fortunate because of how their jaw fits. Paul Winchell had an underbite, and boy, he was able to keep everything still when you looked at his face. If you want to see someone in that caliber with Shari with regard to lip control and facial expression, look up Nina Conte. But Shari holding Lamb Chop basically against her cheek—knowing that people are looking at her mouth—really shows her confidence and her skill level.

—*Lisa Sweazy*

would work. She could get up and work in the mirror, but she was more comfortable working on the bed. It was funny to see her without the puppet—just the hand. She had to figure out how to manipulate her hands to make it look like the puppets were speaking."

In later years, a new writer had just presented a script to Mom for judgment. She was sitting silently reading the script and wiggling her fingers when it was Lamb Chop's line. The writer felt sorry for her and thought she had palsy.

—*Mallory*

Shari was a tough taskmaster when it came to her material, and she was as hard on herself as she was on others. "For any performer," says Brady, summarizing her former boss's attitude, "it's 'I'm the one who has to go out onstage. If it's fucked up, it's not like *it's* fucked up, *I* am.' She's the one who had to do it. She was very hard on herself. I remember somebody once asking me, 'Was it hard working for her because she was demanding?' I said, 'No, it's very easy working for someone who knows exactly what they want.'" Daughter Mallory, who worked on her mother's 1990s TV series, agrees. "It was very easy producing for her. She knew what she wanted."

Says Brady, "If you disagreed and you had a good reason, she understood." Adds Mallory, "If you were right and she didn't want you to be right, she'd say, 'You're not wrong.' Here's the thing. She didn't like being told 'No' if it was *hard* to do, but I had no trouble explaining to her if it's not *possible*. If you're lazy, it's her saying, out of exasperation, 'pedestal [the camera] down, move the camera over there, and I don't care if it's across the line, I want it over my shoulder so the kids can see what my hand is doing.' I found her very easy to work with. You just had to be very good at your job."

The impact of *The Shari Lewis Show* on its young audience had as much to do with her as with her talent. When the series began she was twenty-seven years old, vivacious, and extremely attractive. It's no surprise, then, that an entire generation of Baby Boomers grew up thinking of Shari as a big sister or, for the boys, as a babysitter who sparked their prepubescent fantasies. For the rest of her life, Shari would meet men who confessed that she had been their first crush. How Lamb Chop felt about this is unreported.

"She was the girl next door, the big sister," agrees author Gary H. Grossman. "She was cute, perky, delightful, approachable. She was that person we could be safe with, share stories with, because she shared stories with us. It wasn't like when we saw Annette [Funicello] grow up on television because Annette was becoming a woman; she was hot. I don't think we could describe Shari as hot. She was like a family member."

The Shari Lewis Show was nominated for three Emmys and won the prestigious 1960 Peabody® Award[7] before it was canceled and replaced—confirming Shari's worst fears—by cartoons, specifically, by *The Alvin Show*. An animated program derived from David Seville's (Ross Bagdasarian) smash 1958 recording of "The Chipmunk Song," *The Alvin Show* hit CBS on October 4, 1961, in prime time. This started the clock ticking for Shari and her live-action brethren. One year earlier *The Flintstones* had premiered in prime time on ABC with the dubious premise of being the first cartoon TV series for adults. When adults didn't swallow its low-rent rip-off of *The Honeymooners*, it was banished, along with Alvin and the

7. The Peabody citation reads: "*The Shari Lewis Show*, NBC, is a unique television program in which the talents of Shari Lewis as a singer, dancer, and ventriloquist charm children of all ages. Her clever manipulation of puppets and the never-ceasing rhythmic flow of her presentation create a program of entertaining and cultural values. In recognition, the Peabody Award for TV children's programs." Shari won seven Emmy Awards and was nominated for four more.

Chipmunks, to the Saturday morning children's television ghetto. The tide had turned, and Shari was left high and dry by her demographics.

"You had a chance of getting bigger ratings with animation," says Squire Rushnell, who was in charge of Saturday morning programming for ABC in the mid-1970s. "It sustains better. Over the long haul—and I don't know if anybody's done a study of this—how long did most live-action shows last in the television distribution channels versus how long did animated properties last? I think animated properties had the lead. At least I always went under that assumption." Rushnell, who now writes the successful, inspirational *When God Winks* books, was a friend and a fan of Shari's, but the numbers weren't. "We never really did a show," he continues, "because our Saturday morning schedule was wall-to-wall animation and that was working, so to put a live-action series into that didn't necessarily make sense. And also there was a sense that Shari's [audience] was younger than the six- to twelve-year-olds that we were targeting on ABC Saturday mornings. The feeling was that she was more for the preschool area. I don't know if that was a correct foundation or not, but I loved her and loved her talent and was happy that I got to know her."

Similarly, Margaret Loesch, who has held executive positions at Fox Kids, Jim Henson Entertainment, Marvel, Hanna-Barbera, and Hallmark, always wanted to do a show with Shari but faced the same demographics that daunted Rushnell. "I remember in the 1990s when Shari came to us when I was with Fox," she says. "She had had a successful run on the BBC. All her shows were targeted at preschoolers. She didn't get on Saturday morning TV in the eighties and nineties because we all probably shared the thought that more preschool targeting would garner a preschool audience and we were going for older children. She made the rounds for all the kids' Saturday morning shows. We may have been wrong, to tell you the truth, but I don't think we were wrong because [she] was up against the fast-paced cartoons and action shows."

The personal delivery and slower pacing that made Shari effective to young viewers couldn't compete with the speed of animated shows or with the numbers they were drawing. It seems counterintuitive that television would find animated shows more profitable than live programming; after all, they cost much more to make. But despite a higher initial cost, they can be rerun, syndicated, and repeatedly licensed. Their animated stars never complain, and if the voices behind them become too demanding, they can always be replaced by sound-alikes. The trend would explode by the end of the decade into product-based cartoon series such as *Transformers®*, *He-Man and Masters of the Universe®*, *G.I. Joe®*, *Go-Bots®*, *Hot Wheels®*, and other franchises that, as the FCC declared in 1969, were "designed primarily to promote the sale of a sponsor's product, rather than to serve the public by either entertaining or informing it."

Shari never made product endorsements, but she didn't decline all offers to merchandise her puppets. In the 1960s she allowed the Clarolyte Company to produce a plastic Lamb Chop, but not much else. Thus, when Susan Miller began representing Shari in 1988, they worked together to bring a wider array of child-responsible Lamb Chop products to her young fans. The lunch boxes, coloring books, and children's books were all derived from her characters and not—importantly—the other way around. Yet merchandising and exploitation were a synergy that bothered Shari from the start. "There is a real attitude that says, 'If it sells, it's worth my doing, for, after all, we are only giving people what they want,'" she said sarcastically. "There is a real lack of awareness of the power that we [have] as creators of shows; there's no such thing as 'just entertainment.' A show has a heavy message that it delivers and there are many people out there who are receptive to this particular message. You are changing a child's life when you create a toy; toys are the storytellers of our day. Look what Barbie has told us for years about being a woman. Many people have not thought through what their own message is. If you don't know what your own message is, it's like you're shooting a weapon without knowing if you've got bullets in the gun." It was an ethic that Shari respected throughout her career, even at the expense of business opportunities.

NBC pulled the plug on *The Shari Lewis Show* after the September 28, 1963, episode aired. It hit Shari hard and she took to her bed. "That was the only time I ever went to Lamb Chop and cried with her," she admitted.[8] When her tears dried, she vowed that it would be the last time she would allow herself to indulge in self-pity.

8. Kira Albin, "Shari Lewis in the Lamb Light," *Grandtimes*, 1997, www.grandtimes.com/lambchop.html.

Immediately she began the reinventing process. Five years later, a new *Shari Lewis Show* was picked up by the BBC as a fifteen-minute series. It was produced in England from 1968 to 1975. It troubled Shari that she had to leave America to make TV shows for children, but she took it in stride. She also performed regularly in Canada with the Irish Rovers.

While in England, as might be expected for a visiting American celebrity, Shari and Jeremy were invited to Buckingham Palace, resulting in a story that became a family legend. Shari was in line to meet the royal family when Princess Anne asked, "How did you become a ventriloquist?" Shari responded, "Well, my father was an entertainer," and HRH remarked, "Yes, one does tend to become involved in one's family profession." On another occasion they were at a royal function at which prawns were served. The British custom is to leave the heads of the shellfish on, and as Shari picked one up, Jeremy supposedly put his head in his hands and said to himself, "Dear God, please don't let her make it talk."

I think the statute of limitations has run out on this. Mom got a very large check for performing in England and did not want to pay taxes on it in America, so she cashed the check in England and shoved the money—and I'm talking tens of thousands of dollars—into her bra and underwear and went through customs declaring nothing. When my parents got home, my mother took off her bra and underwear, and all this money fell out. My father asked, "What is that?" She said, "I didn't want to pay double taxes on the money so I cashed the check." He said, "What if they had searched you?" And her response was, "Oh, for Chrissake, Jeremy, who's going to search Shari Lewis's bra?"

—*Mallory*

Between 1963 and 1968 Shari delved into other enterprises in a constant effort to keep her career afloat. Although she was never one to look back, it was important for her to screen the videotapes of her earlier shows for reference. She was horrified to learn what NBC had done to them. "Oh, those monsters," she said. "We were the first show to be taped on Ampex when the good tape came in. We were the first children's show to be taped in color and for the 1964 [presidential] election they called and said to us, 'We need the tape stock; is it okay with you if we transfer these to film?' And of course we said yes because that sounded fine and better for preservation, knowing that tape had its problems. And they changed it to *black-and-white* film!"[9] The UCLA Film and Television Archive now holds and preserves the kinescopes.

There was, however, one significant event during the NBC series that mitigated all the others. Pregnant at the end of 1961, Shari could hide her condition by sitting behind the puppet fence or by cradling Lamb Chop on her arm and being photographed in a tight two-shot. If she had to dance, she did it in a barrel or some other body-covering costume. After one particularly energetic performance of the dance "Jump Up" with Jackie Warner,[10] staffers worried that she might deliver the baby right there on the studio floor. The matter was resolved on July 8, 1962, when she and Jeremy welcomed Mallory Tarcher into the world.

Like her mother, Mallory would be raised around show business. But first, Shari had to stay in it herself.

9. Even after live TV was replaced by videotape, the two-inch tape stock was so expensive that black-and-white film kinescopes were traditionally the cheapest way to preserve shows and recycle the tape. Black-and-white film was more light sensitive and easier to use than color, although a few shows were "kinnied" in color or through an esoteric lenticular process that was equally expensive. The low quality of kinescopes explains why so few early TV shows are rerun today, although many eventually appeared on home video, mostly for collectors. In theory, *The Shari Lewis Show* could be colorized by computer, but it's a question of finance, not technology.

10. Not to be confused with Hollywood studio mogul Jack L. Warner.

7

Home and Office

In a 1994 interview for her mother's episode of A&E's *Biography* series, Mallory jokingly dismissed all thought of competition between herself and Lamb Chop: "People always used to ask me if I was jealous of Lamb Chop. As far as I'm concerned, Lamb Chop is a sock. I'm not jealous of my mother's shoes either. I never had a problem with that. Lamb Chop is the perfect little sister. She works and earns a ton of money, she lives in a shoe box, and she stands to inherit nothing. Who could want a sibling better than that? Kidding. Lamb Chop's my little sister and I love her.

"The truth is, given her druthers, Lamb Chop was probably all the child Mom really wanted," Mallory admits. "She told me once that if it had not been expected of a children's entertainer to have a child, she wouldn't have. My father likely did want children. After all, in the sixties, children had little impact on a dad's career.

"I was a scheduled delivery," she explains. "No, it wasn't a cesarean, it was television. Every woman who had a TV series in those days (and even now) arranged to have their babies in June or July while their shows were on hiatus. Accordingly," she continues, "Mom went into labor on their boat a couple of hours up the Hudson. My dad said, 'That's great, I'll boil water and deliver the baby,' and my mom said, 'No, point the boat toward the hospital and let's go—NOW.'"

Following Mallory's arrival on July 8, 1962, Shari and Jeremy divided their time between raising her and planning for *The Shari Lewis Show* to start up again in September. To help with the baby, Shari hired the first in a succession of nannies, an imperious British woman with the memorable name Miss Head. "She only took babies for six months," recalls Mary Lou Brady with a knowing smile. "Shari said she would feed Mallory before she went to work and she would leave the studio at 5:00, get back to the apartment 5:30 or 6:00, feed her daughter dinner, and spend some time with her." According to Brady, "Miss Head got fired because she said, 'Babies eat at 5:00.' And Shari said, 'Babies eat when I get home.' And Miss Head said, 'Babies eat at 5:00.' And Shari said, 'Not in *my* house.'"

> Mom never hired au pairs. I'd watch this happen so many times as a kid. The mother would bring the child into kindergarten, then she would have another child, and then the nineteen-year-old girl from Sweden who's the au pair would bring the kids to school. Then in third grade there would be the divorce. Why on earth would you bring a nineteen-year-old girl into your home? No, Mom never had au pairs.
>
> —*Mallory*

Shari had no problem juggling motherhood, career, and marriage. The tricky part was the percentage of time she devoted to each. "I think it was difficult," Brady says, "but Shari was not going to be a Hollywood hausfrau. She just wasn't. She loved her child, she loved her husband, she loved her home—but she loved entertaining more. I'm sorry, that's who she was. I think we are all who we are. That was a major part of her personality. She loved it. She loved performing."

Former children's television programming executive Squire Rushnell has the same take on Shari's professional devotion. "Shari was one of those personalities and had the ability to communicate so sweetly with Lamb Chop and her other characters. It transcended any age barrier. Kids could understand it at their level and adults and parents could connect with it on their level. That powerful personality is what I think is gold."

That personality rubbed off on Mallory, who was precocious right from the start. "There were some really hilarious stories," Brady recalls. "Mallory was about three. I remember the nurse—her face, not her name. She would take Mally at breakfast. This was when the show was over and we worked at the home every day. She would take Mally to Central Park to be with other kids. One of them was Sam Robards (son of Lauren Bacall and Jason Robards Jr.), who was four at the time. One day at noon the nurse comes back with Mally. We all go out to the hallway to see the baby coming home. The nurse said, 'She was very naughty today. She got into a fight with another child.' Mally looked at her mother and says, 'She was trying to take my Sam away from me!'"

As the 1960s rolled on and American society was bloodied by war and assassinations, the status of women began to change. In 1960 the birth control pill was approved. In 1962 Betty Friedan's breakthrough book *The Feminine Mystique* was published. More and more women entered the workplace. While some families imploded under the expansion of gender roles, the Tarcher home had long since reached enlightenment. Jeremy had grown up around strong women; his mother was a lawyer and head of the Legal Aid Society. He had always been supportive of Shari; to him, it seemed perfectly normal to have a working wife. (It also helped that she brought in more money from performing than he did from publishing.)

But Shari did not consider herself a pioneer and certainly not a feminist. While women were marching, lobbying, and voting for gender equality, Shari had already attained what they wanted. She was less concerned with women's rights in general than with her own rights and advancing her career. If the two coincided, fine.

Shari compartmentalized her work life and her personal life. She never brought Lamb Chop to any of Mallory's schools to put on a show. "Not once," Mallory says. "It wasn't *productive* to perform at my school." But, she recalls, "my childhood needs were all met. I had people to drive me here and there. I had plenty of food and focused attention from Mom when she wasn't working. I would come home from school and we would hang out for five to ten minutes and then Mom would say, 'Mommy has to go back to work now.' Because she was working at the house, that's no different from working [outside]. It was an office in the house with four or five staff. You wouldn't expect, as a kid, if you dropped by your dad's office after school, for your dad to stop working. In that era, other people's mommies were not working. She had no respect for women who didn't work, and therefore not much respect for the contribution that a non-income-producing mother makes on the child. Mom feared not working; that was how she valued herself. In the case of both of my parents, I was a satellite orbiting the earth." Mallory searches for the right phrase. "I parented differently. I parented my son and always performed at his school. Mom adored me, but parenting was very compartmentalized for her as it was for most of that generation.

"People have often asked me if my mom really loved kids. She respected kids. She certainly liked them in the normal way any adult likes kids, but she had no interest in hanging out with other people's children. Then again, what kind of creepy adult does like to hang out with other people's children? Mom loved being a children's entertainer but, given her choice, she would have been a performer for adults."

Jeremy was also largely absent, but that's because, as Mallory says, "he was working. He was in publishing. The shows were produced by Tarcher Productions but he never had a personal credit." Susan Miller agrees. "He was hardly involved in the business at all. He was just someone who was kind and helpful. Occasionally we would have a creative discussion and he would be with [Shari] if he was in New York. He really didn't come to meetings. It's more like we would socialize together when I went out. We would go out to dinner. It was her business."

Mary Lou Brady (who by this point had become a family friend as well as an employee) concurs: "They had a great relationship from the inside and the outside. Obviously later on things changed, but I saw a happy marriage and I saw people who worked together on certain projects. They talked over things. I never saw anything other than that it was pretty solid."

It would take such solidarity to face the years after *The Shari Lewis Show* was canceled. Having lost access to regular national exposure, Shari was determined to keep herself before the public eye.

In show business, nobody ever takes you aside and says, "It's over," but Shari could read the writing on the dressing room wall and later acknowledged, "In each case you can feel it happening." Quickly she changed gears and decided that this was an opportunity. In hindsight, she proclaimed, "I like variety. I think if I had done the same thing all through my life I'd have been burned out like my friends are burned out."

With Jeremy just getting started in publishing (he would soon make a success with books by Phyllis Diller and Buddy Hackett), Shari, too, became an author. Her first book, published in 1962, was *Folding Paper Puppets,* for which her writing partner was origami expert Lillian Oppenheimer. Unlike the copyright registration for Lamb Chop, her book and video copyright listings credit her collaborators such as Oppenheimer, Lan O'Kun, and Jackie Reinach. The books became another phase of her career.

"She was always reinventing herself," says Brady. "Even when she didn't have the schedule of the weekly TV show, there was always something to do. She wrote books, wrote the origami books.[1] I was the guinea pig. She would write the instructions for origami and I would have to do it. She figured if I could do it, an eight-year-old could."

"One of the leading characteristics of her personality," Jeremy said (speaking with Shari sitting beside him), "is her focus and concentration on one thing and then another thing and then the next thing. There is an indomitableness of spirit that has grown as Shari has become a person of extraordinary calm over the course of the years. I've read all the [self-help] books and she is the one who has become calm. We don't know quite how that happens. That, I think, is very important to the whole sense of who she is." Turning to Shari, he said, "I don't know, darling, if you want to talk about those insecurities you share with other performers, the need for acceptance and recognition, the riskiness of the work." Then he reset his focus. "Shari's life has always been governed by homilies from her upbringing to a greater degree than anybody I know. She integrates a lot of her childhood wisdom: 'The day begins the night before'—she is ready to start each day because she has, indeed, prepared herself for the next day in every way she knows how. 'Have faith and be of good courage'—Shari has kept her sense of faith in herself and courageousness, particularly during a slow spell—twenty years from the early sixties to the late eighties—during which each year she kept producing that product, which is herself, until PBS was there to put her back on the air in 1991." In fact, the epitaph on her memorial bench is "Not for Want of Trying."

Shari and Jeremy were an unusual couple, mismatched in some ways, but also complementary. "Jeremy knew everything," says writer-producer Gary H. Grossman, who became a personal friend. "He was very much a renaissance man and philosophical and thoughtful and deep. On any given day I aspire to be one of those things, but never all three. He was an encyclopedia of mythology, folklore, history, art. At meals I recall it settled on what Jeremy wanted to do. I listened intently. We took a trip

1. Shari Lewis and Lillian Oppenheimer, *Folding Paper Puppets* (New York: Stein & Day, 1962); Shari Lewis and Lillian Oppenheimer, *Folding Paper Toys* (New York: Stein & Day, 1963); Shari Lewis, *Folding Paper Masks* (New York: Dutton, 1965).

with them to Santa Fe, New Mexico, and went to the [art] galleries. [Shari] was very appreciative of the art and the artists. She would spend time with them; of course, most people would recognize her. I don't think she was 'on,' I think she was sincere. She was always appreciative of other people's artistry. Jeremy was a heavier soul, a real warm and welcoming nature. He would speak softly and slowly while Shari was this bundle of energy. She also gave me the best bit of philosophy, and not a week goes by that I don't share it. I asked her, 'Shari, you're conducting eighteen, thirty, forty symphony orchestras around the country; you're writing eight and ten books a year; you have your TV show and you're overseeing the production of your merchandising. How do you do all this?' And she looked at me with a slight twinkle in her eye and said, 'Gary, how do you eat an elephant?' It took me a moment to realize the answer: one bite at a time. It's an old African saying. Forever I will thank Shari for that because I tell people that when I teach."

I'm a runner, and Shari knew I was a runner. One day I came into the house to go over some stuff that she wanted me to write and she said, "Sonny, I am so proud of myself. Jeremy and I ran from the house all the way to Rodeo Drive," about a mile and a half. "Wow," I said, "that's great. So all told you did a mile and a half up and a mile and a half back? That's three miles." She said, "Oh, no, we caught a cab back."

—*Sonny Gordon*

Even in the slow period of the mid-1960s, Shari continued the tight scheduling that had impressed Jeremy on their first date. Mindful that learning to type, cook, drive a car, or do office work would yoke her to traditional women's jobs from which the Women's Movement was struggling to emerge, Shari set her own rules for others to observe. She kept her life in order and expected others, even family, to respect it. Although she was sociable, she had no time to simply hang out with friends. "She was working from the age of three," Mallory says. "She loved my dad and she loved work and I loved working with her. It was an honor. I'm a morning person and would come to the house before seven. Dad said not to come before 7:00 a.m. Mom disagreed, and as usual, Mom won." She wouldn't schedule meetings at quarter-hour intervals; she limited them to ten minutes. She refused to learn how to drive, so other people would have to come to her, saving herself from time-consuming commutes and participation in school carpools.

"She never learned to drive because she always wanted to be working in the car," confirms television producer Sonny Fox. Fox captured young audiences in the early 1960s as host of the four-hour *Wonderama* TV show on Sunday mornings, on which Shari was a guest. "She was a person who was perpetually working and never stopped. Her energies never flagged." Affectionately calling her the "peripatetic puppeteer," Fox adds, "she thought driving was a waste of time. Always working, always, and always seemed to be rushed. She was always taking notes or doing something in the car while she was being driven as opposed to sitting back and relaxing and laughing. That was not in her makeup."

> Driving seems to have been a family curse. It was something that ran in the family, especially with her father, Abe. When he'd be driving he would get lost in his head and thoughts, talking to Ann, and it wouldn't be unlikely for him to stop in the middle of a freeway to turn and respond. As Shari said, in her early days of going to studios, she used the cab time to focus on her work and getting her voice in order, and even to change clothes in the backseat. She never had the kind of focus to drive herself. It wouldn't be safe and it wouldn't make any sense.
>
> —*Todd Tillson*

But there was a price to pay on the home front. Whenever Mallory took sick, Shari would wait at the doorway of her daughter's bedroom while Georgia Anderson, the Tarchers' housekeeper, carried in the chicken soup. Shari couldn't risk coming down with whatever Mallory had, lest it force her to miss a show. She always stood at the door and chatted, but she was a bit of a germophobe.

"The other thing Mom knew," says Mallory, "was that people would always come to you if you fed them, so there was always hot and cold running food in our house. Mom had the benefit of staff, but I could no more have people at the house and not have food and things than

I could meet you at the door naked with a clown wig on. In fact, that's more likely. She always hosted a good meeting."

Every performer with a career of any length spends a certain amount of time in the wilderness, and Shari was no different. Says Mallory, "She wrote sixty books during that time period, she learned how to conduct symphony orchestras, she did a lot of fairs." When her regular series work stopped, she drew on her other talents to keep herself before the public, often without Lamb Chop. Far from breaking up the act, it broadened her appeal, even though every new booking was a struggle.

8

On the Road

Jeremy's publishing career was taking off in the 1960s. Much of it was due to Shari; she introduced him to many of the celebrities whose books became the backbone of Tarcher Press, such as Buddy Hackett and Phyllis Diller. His company's success attracted interest from Stein & Day, a conventional publisher looking to acquire a progressive imprint.

Tarcher Press "had already been incorporated as Stein & Day," reports Mary Lou Brady, who had been working with Jeremy's company and was present for the intended union. "He invested *X* number of dollars and they were setting up the office. He asked me to come help them for a week and I said sure. At the end of the week I said to Jeremy, 'There isn't enough money in the world for me to work for Sol Stein, the son of a bitch.' He treated you like shit. Sol Stein went through secretaries one a month. When Jeremy started to go to the office every day, he began to realize, 'This is not what I want.' He and Sol had disagreements. Jeremy was gonna pull back and they would repay him his investment [in installments]. Every month the check would come in, maybe the fifth or sixth of the month. Now we get to a month when it's the seventh day. Jeremy is looking at me. The eighth day. Then the ninth day. Jeremy and I are hysterical; how could he be so stupid? After the tenth day [Stein is] in default on the contract, and at that point, did Sol think Jeremy wouldn't go after him to fulfill his obligation? The hilarity was that Jeremy and I would count the days. That was a difficult time. He was looking to establish himself."

The merger was called off acrimoniously, and Jeremy was unmoored both professionally and spiritually.

At the same time, Shari was on the road, appearing in summer stock and national touring companies of the hit musicals *Damn Yankees; Bye,*

Bye, Birdie; and *Funny Girl.* She also toured for twelve weeks in 1963 with Darren McGavin and Guy Madison in the play *The Indoor Sport.* Despite turning down an appearance on the prestigious *Ed Sullivan Show* in 1960 because the controlling Sullivan refused to let her perform without her puppets, they later worked out their differences, and Shari was on his immensely popular Sunday night variety program six times between 1960 and 1965. She even reunited with Arthur Godfrey in two 1963 specials, *Arthur Godfrey Loves Animals* and his Thanksgiving variety hour. She and Lamb Chop guested on *Missing Links, Get the Message, The Match Game, Hollywood Squares, Tattletales, Fanfare,* and other game shows. Since this was the golden age of variety television, she was welcomed by Dean Martin, Bob Hope, Joey Bishop, Jack Paar, Johnny Carson, Merv Griffin, and Danny Kaye. She cohosted with Mike Douglas in Philadelphia for a week in 1965.

Shari's November 11, 1964, appearance on *The Danny Kaye Show* required some last-minute restaging when the versatile Kaye badly sprained his foot during rehearsal and had to tape the show from a wheelchair. Tony Charmoli was the choreographer of the ballet that Shari was supposed to perform with Kaye while Lamb Chop did color commentary. "Danny said, 'I can do the show if I can keep my foot up'—he's all in a cast and bandaged—and indeed he came and did the show," Charmoli told the Television Academy. "I said, 'Shari will start with you sitting down and singing the song and you sing with her, we'll put her on this side, and then the minute you finish the song she steps in with me and I'll do the dancing with her, and then we'll end the song and she'll dance over to you again and finish the song with you.' And that's how we did the number. [Danny] said [to the audience], 'That was supposed to be me out there, but it was Tony.'"[1]

The Hollywood Palace was another Shari showcase. She wanted to do it sans Lamb Chop but, like Sullivan, the producers insisted that the puppet make at least a brief appearance. The January 21, 1967, episode of *Hollywood Palace* was hosted by Donald O'Connor, with whom she had just worked in Las Vegas. Following Lamb Chop's perfunctory cameo on

1. Tony Charmoli, interviewed by Sunny Parich, December 12, 1997, for Television Academy.com.

O'Connor's shoulder, Shari sang "I Want to Dance with Fred Astaire" and then proceeded to do just that—not the actual Fred Astaire, of course, but a life-sized dummy elegantly dressed in top hat and tails and fastened to her body in such a way that she moved for both of them. The effect was stunning.

"Fred" was built by puppeteer Ralph Lee, to whom Shari had been referred by famed costumer Ray Deffen. Says Lee (who now heads the Metawee River Theatre Festival in upstate New York), "She would often need props or some kind of costume effects to put on her puppets. She called me up and I'd usually have overnight to do it because the show was going to tape the next day. I made a snowsuit for Lamb Chop, various things. Then she asked me to do this Fred Astaire thing. She was going to be branching out and had some kind of a show in Las Vegas. It was the first time and the last time I ever made anything like that."

The rig was more complicated than the audience could see. For one thing, like Ginger Rogers, Shari had to dance backwards. Then there were the mechanics. "One of her shoes attached to one of Fred Astaire's shoes so she got that simultaneous stepping," Lee explains, "and then one of her arms held the arm of Fred Astaire and the other arm was a fake arm that went around his back. Her real arm went into the puppet so that she could move his head. I made it as light as I could, but it still weighed something."

"That thing weighed a ton," says Mary Lou Brady, who had to work out its travel logistics. "We had Fred in New York. It was hilarious to travel with him because he was six feet long and it was like traveling with a corpse. That thing weighed, what, forty–fifty pounds. Half of her weight. To dance with that thing, to have the feet attached and to maneuver with

---

There is a family story that Mom was clearing customs into England and the customs officials opened the "Fred coffin" and saw Fred's body with a cloth over his face and the extra pair of shoes (my dad's) Mom had tucked into the case. Supposedly the customs agent said, "Oh, the poor dear won't need these anymore." I'm not sure if it really happened, but it's a great story.

—*Mallory*

She had a case that Fred sat in. It was a little spooky having that case in my studio. If I walked in at night, I suddenly realized that I had this body there.

—*Ralph Lee*

After Mom died, I had Fred Astaire sitting in a chair in my office, which doubles as a guest room. Whenever we had guests, I would come in and find that someone had put their underwear or at the very least a towel over Fred's face, as they didn't want him watching them have sex! I finally traded Fred Astaire to a wonderful performer named Miss Tina, a magician at the Magic Castle. She was exactly Mom's size and did a fabulous quick-change outfit for Fred. She was also a wonderful dancer and knew how to sew. I traded Fred for slip covers for my couch.

—*Mallory*

the hands, was extraordinary." Brady recalls, "When she left New York she would still ask me to connect her shoe to the Fred Astaire shoe because her shoes would stretch a certain amount so she would need to get a new one of her shoes to put onto Fred Astaire's shoes. I would get her old shoe and the Fred Astaire shoe in the mail and I would send her a new one."

Fred was only a fling; Shari and Lamb Chop were a team. One of their more unusual appearances occurred on *The Jack Benny Program* on March 18, 1962. In an instance of art hinting at life, Jack's producer tells him that he has to cut one of the acts from his show, and he decides to axe Shari Lewis. When he tries to break the news to Shari and Lamb Chop, however, he becomes so charmed by their versatility that he bumps all the other performers and partners solely with them. During the program, Shari sings "I Want to Be a Song and Dance Man," does magic, plays the violin, and winds up accompanying Benny on piano (!) while he takes up the fiddle and performs—in his distinctive, screechy way—"Alabamy Bound."

According to Shari, the Benny booking grew out of their working together in Las Vegas. "I opened for Jack," she said. "He had shingles and he was really a fabulous trouper and he kept going. Lamb Chop and he did eleven minutes together onstage, which was quite thrilling for me, but I could see him sinking as the engagement went on and I kept thinking, 'I'm going to be the one that kills Jack Benny onstage.' Finally he had to back out and Frank Gorshin took over. Very sad."

"I was very fortunate that I had long-term contracts with the Sahara in Las Vegas and Lake Tahoe," she told interviewer Kira Albin of *Grandtimes* in 1997, remembering her fallow spell. "Although it was extremely difficult to know that my entire field had crashed around my ears, it was very interesting to move into the casinos. I opened for Jack Benny and Donald O'Connor and many other wonderful stars. It was also devastating. The only bout with depression that I've ever had was at that period."

Jeremy chronicles her odyssey during this difficult time. "She did symphonic conducting. Personal appearances. She made a living as an author. She made her living in five or six or perhaps seven different aspects of the business, and when one thing was exhausted or began to diminish in productivity, she had the strength to go on to the next one. This constant reeducation, refocusing, was what kept her going."

One particular enterprise in late 1968 opened a new frontier for both Shari and Jeremy. Eager to display her dramatic chops, and aware that *Star Trek* was one of the few television series that accepted story ideas from outsiders, the couple pitched "The Lights of Zetar" to the science fiction series, which was heading into its third season. By this time, however, the show's creator, Gene Roddenberry, had more or less walked off after a snit with the network over a new time slot. Then Paramount, which had acquired the show's production company, Desilu, tightened the budget as the ratings dropped, even though *Trek* fans were mounting another effort to save the series. With newly assigned producer Fred Freiberger buffeted by studio infighting, the decision was made to reject Shari in the starring role in her own script and cast Jan Shutan, an actress roughly Shari's age, who had appeared on the doctor series *Ben Casey*.

In "The Lights of Zetar" (air date January 31, 1969; star dates 5725.3–5725.6), the USS *Enterprise* encounters an energy force that is bent on erasing the Federation's research facility on the planet Memory Alpha. Lieutenant Mira Romaine (Shutan) forms a psychic link with the force, which turns out to be the population of the dead world Zetar, who converted themselves into energy and went in search of a new home. Captain

Kirk persuades Lieutenant Romaine to allow the force to inhabit her, then encloses her in a special chamber that euthanizes the Zetans while leaving her untouched. Romaine then takes up residence on Memory Alpha to spend her life restoring the facility. In the meantime, she has an abbreviated affair with the ship's engineer, Lieutenant Commander Montgomery "Scotty" Scott.

Though she was denied an acting opportunity, at least Shari and Jeremy received sole writing credit, even though it was fairly well known throughout Trekdom that several others, including Roddenberry, Gene Coon, and D. C. (Dorothy) Fontana, routinely rewrote nearly everything. That episode is one of the few that features a romance with any *Enterprise* crew member other than Captain Kirk, not to mention a shocking case of genocide (the entire Zetan population) and an introduction to the notion of digital information storage.

> Arguably the most boring of all *Star Trek* episodes, "Memory Alpha" is, to this day, the name of the *Star Trek* Wiki site.
>
> —*Mallory*

"I see it all on a continuum," Shari stated in retrospect. "When I write a book I'm just putting my performance between covers. When I conduct, it's entertainment through classical music. I was brought up to be an entertainer. My father used to insist that, whatever I did, I would take at least a week of training, eight hours a day, and then I didn't have to continue. So I studied juggling for a week with Larry Weeks, who's one of the great jugglers of all time. Now, I'm very nearsighted and when that ball is up in the air I'm going like this [she squints]. I can't see the baton.

> Oddly, decades later, Shari's grandson Jamie Hood (then seven) said virtually the same thing to his mom after baseball practice. "I don't get baseball," he said. "You stand in a cage holding a stick and people throw balls at your head." Clearly genetics at play.
>
> —*Mallory*

After a week I said, 'This is silly. If you throw it at me, I'm gonna duck.' I never played a ball game in my life; if you want the ball, you can have it."

If Shari was wandering in the show business wilderness in the late 1960s and early 1970s, she was not alone. So was children's television. At this point in her career, she had not yet decided to concentrate on "edutainment," but she was being battered by the same forces that were placing an entire generation of young people at risk.

To recap: when commercial television first appeared in 1948, it did so at the crack of noon in most major cities, if not later. With barely 325,000 TV sets in use nationwide, compared to 65 million radios, there was simply no audience. By 1949, the number of TV sets had increased tenfold, and the Baby Boom audience was eager to be weaned on what author Harlan Ellison would later call "the glass teat." Children's television initially occupied the weekday afternoon time slot between 4:00 p.m., when kids got home from school, and 6:00 p.m., when their mothers, as was the domestic arrangement, put dinner on the table. Children's programming was almost an afterthought to the programmers, but not to Shari.

"When her show was first on the air, it was groundbreaking because there was so little available in the genre of children's entertainment," notes Ranny Levy, founder and president of Kids First: Coalition for Quality Children's Television, a group that advocates critical thinking among young viewers. "Her show was geared to young children whose parents watched it with them. It wasn't such segmented viewing as there is today. You came home from school and your mom was there to supervise your after-school play. With more and more working mothers, kids came home and were latchkey kids. They weren't allowed to go out and play because it wasn't the safe thing to do."

More than radio, television became the great babysitter, and the only thing that seemed to concern parents in those days was eyesight: "Don't sit so close to the TV. Do you want to go blind?" As it happened, the blindness wouldn't be optical; it would be judgmental, for television quickly emerged as a hypnotic tool to compel kids to want anything they saw pitched at them and to nag their parents to buy it. At first, there were no rules preventing the live hosts of kiddie shows from doing commercials for foods, toys, restaurants, and all manner of other goods, just as emcees and celebrities did for adult-oriented products on prime-time programming.

At first, it was the local TV stations that catered to kids, usually by tapping somebody from the announcing staff to don makeup and become "Uncle So-and-So" to the boys and girls "out there in television land." Rarely were they as inventive as Soupy Sales or as diligent as Sonny Fox, whose New York City popularity carried them to national prominence. Mostly they were put-upon staffers such as cowboy Pick Temple (Bob Dalton) in Washington, DC, Officer Don (Don Kennedy) in Atlanta, Happy Herb in Indianapolis, Rex Trailer in Boston, Sailor Bob in South Carolina, and scores of others.

What happened next was predictable. As more and more TV sets populated America, sponsors and broadcasters realized they could make more money catering to adults, so children's programming was shifted to Saturday mornings. Custom-produced Saturday morning series didn't appear until ABC debuted *Animal Clinic* and *Acrobat Ranch* on August 19, 1950. NBC followed later that year by showing children's films, and CBS climbed aboard on October 14 with *Us Kids*. It was no tidal wave, which is why it took an act of bravery for the producers of *Wild Bill Hickok, Sky King, Fury, Ramar of the Jungle, Rin-Tin-Tin, The Lone Ranger, Sergeant Preston of the Yukon,* and other fondly remembered series to put them on the air. Shari's 1960–1963 show became part of that tradition. "It was a new technology," Levy says. "There was *Captain Kangaroo, Howdy Doody,* and *Romper Room* for younger kids. There weren't a lot of choices. So it was pretty easy to get your own market share."

All the live-action youth shows experienced the same fate as had Shari and Lamb Chop at the paws of chipmunks and their animated brethren. By the time *The Shari Lewis Show* ended in the mid-1960s, so had the heyday of human characters. The chipmunk invasion was followed by the likes of *The Herculoids®*, *Space Ghost®*, *Moby Dick and the Mighty Mightor®*, *Casper the Friendly Ghost®*, *The Super Six®*, and a host of Marvel comic book heroes with none of the wit of their paper counterparts. "There just aren't any role models for kids today," lamented Peter Graves, the star of *Fury* (and later host of the A&E *Biography* episode about Shari). "I think it's a shame. I don't watch an awful lot of Saturday morning television, but what I've seen comes right off the drawings boards and I don't like it."[2]

For her part, Shari called Saturday morning television "ghastly,"[3] but she persevered. After all, she had a menagerie to support. And support it she did, but as the work changed in the late 1960s, so did Shari. "Everything was animation," she sighs. "There was simply no live entertainment unless you count Pee-Wee Herman, and I don't know if that describes him."

While children's TV was coming apart during this period, so was American society. Some people fought to hold on to a cherished past that no longer existed. Others were bent on revolutionizing the world. Still others ventured into a New Age. Shari Lewis herself was caught in the vortex of all these challenges, and so was her marriage.

2. Gary H. Grossman, *Saturday Morning TV* (New York: Dell, 1981).
3. Grossman.

9

Doody's Revenge

"It was a lot easier talking to the real people than it would have been, years later, interviewing just cartoon characters," says Gary H. Grossman, whose 1981 book *Saturday Morning TV* was the first reference work on the subject. While writing it, he was able to interview most of the pillars of children's TV while they were still alive and lucid. "In the earliest days, the heroes on TV were real," he continues. "They were Roy Rogers, they were Captain Midnight, they were cowboys and spacemen and detectives and crime fighters, and it was great and I got to talk with most of the people that I grew up with, chief among them Roy Rogers, Clayton Moore the Lone Ranger, and, in the children's puppet works, Buffalo Bob Smith and Shari Lewis. They were all working in something brand new. They were very young to begin with, and they were like kids in a candy store."

Live hosts were key to the success of early children's television, and their absence today is a void that cartoons simply cannot fill. "A live host can, like a good radio announcer or disc jockey, talk one-to-one with the viewer," Grossman notes, "even if there's a peanut gallery or something else going on in the studio. In that close-up shot, Shari Lewis was talking to me, Gary Grossman, from Hudson, New York. She was still in that close-up shot talking to me. Children's programming may get noisy and unrelatable, but in its early years it was a close-up medium and it was there for us."

By the late 1960s, however, cartoons had almost completely replaced live hosts across the children's television landscape. Shari Lewis had been one of the first to go, and once her personal depression lifted, the professional in her returned to the starting line.

"Paddy Chayefsky said, 'If you are going to have an enduring career, you have to be ready to go out of fashion a lot,'" Shari reasoned, quoting the writer of *Marty, Network,* and *The Hospital.* "Because nothing is consistent, and what happened was, I replaced and pushed off the air *Howdy Doody.* Then cartoons, namely Chipmunks [*The Alvin Show*], replaced me and pushed me off the air."

The revolution was, in fact, televised. "I remember writing some of the early scripts for *Howdy Doody,* reports Steve Krantz, "which was on every day on the NBC network and that was five days a week. And then they decided that children's programs were not being very commercially suitable and they replaced them with talk shows and things of that [nature], and then consigned them to the weekends. And then they reversed their fields and now cartoons are all over the schedule Monday through Friday, Saturday and Sunday."[1]

Ervin Duggan, former president and CEO of the Public Broadcasting Service (PBS), agrees: "The networks quickly discovered that, particularly the preschool audience, was not a commercial audience. Preschoolers did not buy products, and they were not yet skilled at nagging their parents to buy products, and so, over time, the preschool audience was abandoned."[2] Until 1969, that is, when toys took over television.

Buffalo Bob might have personally hawked Hostess baked goods to his enraptured *Howdy Doody* audience, but Doodyville never had a talking Twinkie living there. Outside of commercials, television networks avoided mentioning brand names in their programs, even going so far as to create generic props. But this was less out of a concern for ethical purity and more to avoid alienating sponsors. Product placement in children's programs, as in adult fare, was pretty much limited to showing the hosts enjoying Post or Kellogg's cereal or whatever item the show was "brought to you by." Nobody ever considered doing *The Snap, Crackle, and Pop Adventure Hour.*

That changed drastically in the late 1960s when toy manufacturers got into the act. In 1969 ABC began airing *Hot Wheels* on Saturday mornings, a half-hour animated series about high school student Jack "Rabbit" Wheeler and his exploits in the Hot Wheels Racing Club.

1. Since 1994, when this interview was conducted, cartoons have spread to cable and streaming.

2. Ervin Duggan, interviewed in 1994.

Not surprisingly, the racing cars and assorted accoutrements were "sold separately" from other toys manufactured by Mattel, the show's prime sponsor. *Hot Wheels* aired from 1969 to 1971, during which time it drew fire—astonishingly—not from parents but from competing toy manufacturers that complained to the FCC that *Hot Wheels* was a program-length commercial designed to sell Mattel toys—which it obviously was. The FCC, in response, demanded not that the show disclose this to the public but that stations log a portion of its running time as advertising rather than entertainment.[3] When President Ronald Reagan took office in 1981 he appointed Marc S. Fowler chairman of the FCC, with a mandate to deregulate broadcasting. Among Fowler's acts was to eliminate the Fairness and Equal Time Doctrines and—more destructively for children's broadcasting—to dissolve the barrier between sponsors and content. The result was an onslaught of product-based kids' shows such as *He-Man and Masters of the Universe, Go-Bots, Transformers, My Little Pony*®, and *She-Ra*®, among many others. They were all cartoons, with their low-quality animation produced in Korea or Japan, but the producers made sure their characters were well represented in American toy stores.

The barrage of show-length commercials was so massive that Peggy Charren, a firebrand activist-housewife from Newton, Massachusetts, founded Action for Children's Television (ACT) in 1968 to "encourage diversification in children's television offerings, to discourage over commercialization of children's programming, and to eliminate deceptive advertising aimed at young viewers."[4] ACT's first targets were violent children's shows such as *Space Ghost, Herculoids,* and *The Fantastic Four.* In 1970 the group urged the FCC to ban advertising entirely from children's television. ACT also recommended at least fourteen hours of children's

3. Interestingly, even in the era when sponsors paid for entire shows and had their names in the title (e.g., *The Colgate Comedy Hour, Philco Playhouse, Kraft Music Hall*), none of them ever based an episode around toothpaste, a TV set, or Velveeta, respectively. They kept their brands strictly in the commercials. They did, however, occasionally censor content, such as when sponsor Southern California Gas Company forbade *Playhouse 90* from showing a gas chamber in a drama about a murderer who was executed.

4. Loree Gerdes Bykerk and Ardith Maney, *U.S. Consumer Interest Groups: Institutional Profiles* (Westport, CT: Greenwood, 1995).

programming each week, the elimination of vitamin ads aimed at children, and a cutback on ads for sugar-laden products.

Needless to say, ACT and Charren were fans of Shari. "Shari Lewis really knows where children are at," Charren said in later years. "She really knows the age group she's talking to. And she's an extraordinarily talented performer. When she puts on her puppet gloves she really becomes the character that she's talking to. But she never loses that sense of what's important to say out loud, what's important to tell kids. And it comes through and kids relate to it. My children loved Lamb Chop, but maybe they didn't love her quite as much as I loved Lamb Chop. She has an ability to reach through all age groups, I think, with those puppets, which is very unusual. In large part it's because of what she says and who Shari Lewis really is."[5]

ACT's efforts to reform children's television would result in passage of the Children's Television Act of 1990. Back in the late 1960s, however, Shari's only option was scrambling for guest appearances on game shows or variety shows. She also faced a moral dilemma: how to exploit her creations without tarnishing them—how to sell without selling out.

"You want to know what Shari has that's special as opposed to anybody else?" Steve Krantz asks. "She has a sense of honor, which is really at the heart of what she feels is right for children. She's never pandered, she's never sunk to the level beneath what children have the right to expect. She's always given them a sense of growth and enlargement as opposed to reducing their lives. The children's entertainment, principally, except for *Sesame Street* and a few other shows, is really diminishing those kids' lives. Shari has always expanded them."

"When we were on television back in those days," says Sonny Fox, "the parents were still asleep. There was nothing for the kids to do except watch television, so they tuned us in in huge numbers because we were the only alternative. When a kid watches television now, the critical thing is that he has the [remote] in his or her hand. When I was doing it, he had to get up off the sofa and turn the dial to get rid of me. That changed a lot of things in terms of how we paced shows."

5. Peggy Charren, interviewed in 1994.

Faced with competition from a changing industry, Shari again reinvented herself. Between 1976 and 1982 she turned to doing specials for the Canadian Broadcasting Corporation (CBC), starting with *Christmas with Shari Lewis* (1977), a variety hour. Mindful of her prior experience with Ed Sullivan (who refused to let her appear without her puppets), she carefully balanced Lamb Chop with solo work. In *Shari's Christmas Concert* (1981) she danced with two life-sized chorus girl figures attached to her body, similar to her pas de deux with the faux Fred Astaire on *The Hollywood Palace*. Heavier than "Fred," the dummy duo looped around her neck and she operated them from behind. "Sharp-eyed observers can see that she had them made with thicker legs than hers so hers would look skinnier," Mallory reveals. "These puppets weighed so much that it pinched her ulnar nerve, paralyzing her for several days afterward."

"They were made for the stage," says Pat Brymer, who created the second set of "the girls." "Usually stage floors are black, and the rods that connected them are black so you don't really notice, especially when it's a long shot. People are amazed that the puppets were doing the same thing [Shari] was doing. First time she premiered them was at Disneyland on the stage in Tomorrowland, where they later had the Michael Jackson 3-D movie [in 1986]. Then she started taking them on the road in her stage shows."

Shari also made countless appearances on other people's variety and game shows, usually as herself, and almost always with Lamb Chop. The list is indicative of both her perseverance in keeping herself in front of the viewing public and the wealth of opportunities offered by the three (that's right, just three) television networks:

Break the Bank
Rhyme and Reason
Dinah! (Dinah Shore)
Musical Chairs
Show-offs
The Tonight Show Starring Johnny Carson
Tattletales
The David Nixon Show
Tony Orlando and Dawn
A Picture of Us (TV movie)

Dinah's Place (Dinah Shore)
Nana Mouskouri
The Mouse Factory (Disney)
The Spinners
Saturday Variety
It's Lulu
Maggie's Place
The Barbara McNair Show
Playboy after Dark
Della (Della Reese)
The Val Doonican Show
The David Frost Show
The Game Donika
Philbin's People
The Royal Variety Performance 1969
Decidedly Dusty
It's Your Bet
Dee Time
You're Putting Me On
It Takes Two
Win with the Stars
You Don't Say
Cilla
What's My Line
The John Gary Show
The Beautiful Phyllis Diller Show
The Joey Bishop Show
The Hollywood Squares (daytime)
George Jessel's Here Come the Stars
The Kraft Music Hall
The Hollywood Palace
The Merv Griffin Show

Between television gigs, Shari wrote a "Kids-Only" column six days a week that ran in five Canadian newspapers. She also continued with her orchestral conducting, but it was all piecework. Although she made repeated appearances on *Della, Tattletales,* and *The Tonight Show,* they were always as herself and always as a specialty act. It wasn't the same as having her own show, but at least it was work.

"Children's programming and Shari Lewis have had an ebb-and-flow that's really interesting," offers Steve Krantz, "and during the times when

Shari was less in vogue, she always found a way to be occupied and be productive. Shari is without doubt one of the most multitalented people I've ever known, and if she's not doing one thing she's doing another. She's preparing, she works, she writes, she composes, she dances, she sings—all of those things are part of her life. And during the times that were dry in terms of not being on the air as often as she used to be, she would do things in Atlantic City or in Las Vegas, do conducting and things of that sort. She would never stop working and she always had the sense that, somehow or other, things would return to allow her to do the things she does best."

"She really wasn't interested in anything other than work," concludes Mary Lou Brady. "She'd go on vacation and have a script with her. That may go back to Abe, being productive—not lying down contemplating your navel."

Shari's skills were so varied that she and her agent could pitch her as the solution to almost any programming need. The problem was that most producers wanted Lamb Chop too. That was a negotiation. There was only one thing she refused to do: county fairs. This was the result of an unnerving experience one year at the Los Angeles County Fair, where the performance area was a barnlike exhibition building with such poor acoustics and so much background noise that Shari had to shout to be heard. (Ironically, fairs are one of Mallory's most popular venues today, thanks to more advanced microphone and sound systems.)

In 1975 there was an ambitious but doomed attempt at a nine-episode dramatic series created by the Tarchers called *The Shari Show.* Set at a television station beset by ratings issues (it has been called *The Mary Tyler Moore Show* with puppets), it took occasional digs at the industry that had tried to write Shari off. It placed Shari in a world of puppets, all of whom she voiced, including "Captain Person" (an homage to Captain Kangaroo) as the station manager. Conceptually, it was a cousin to *The Muppet Show,* which was launched at about the same time and outlasted it by 111 episodes. Jeremy was the show's producer, but only nominally, as Mallory told Maria Carter of *Country Living* magazine in 2017: "My father was an unsuccessful television producer and my mom was the toast of New York City. He was creative and she enjoyed having him as a sounding board and contributor [but] she was in charge because the matter of fact was it was her ass on stage." Mallory calls the marriage "nothing short of a miracle" and marvels that it survived cancer, Jeremy's drug use, and a volatile entertainment industry, all during "a really interesting time in our nation's social history."[6]

In an attempt to keep up with the times, Shari even brought Lamb Chop to Las Vegas—a city that was, in those days, America's playland of booze, chorus girls, gambling, and sin. It's hard to fathom that, with no TV work on the horizon, Shari dipped Lamb Chop's hooves into the adult waters of Las Vegas. Back in the 1980s, the city was not known for its family values (unless it was a crime family), but none of that fazed Shari, who advised reporters that her act would be rated "somewhere between PG and R."[7] Like Disney, she never thought of herself as strictly a children's act but as more of a general audience entertainer, and she never worked "blue."[8]

My favorite memories with my mom were during the Vegas years. From the old car barn in Reno to playing keno after her second show, I loved our "alone time" on the road. I remember her sitting on the bathroom sink to put on her makeup because her vision was so bad and she was too short to get close enough to the mirror. I remember our daily outings (after a late wake-up and before our pre-show nap). Those were great times.

—*Mallory*

"I change the content and the context when I'm performing in Vegas or Atlantic City," she said at the time. "Lamb Chop would be the same Lamb Chop but she would have different aspirations." In one sketch, for example, Lamb Chop appeared drunk, not intentionally but as a result of "massaging her tongue" with an alcoholic beverage. "I'm never vulgar," Shari assured, "but the last time I played there, the reviews said

6. *Country Living*, June 30, 2017.

7. Janet Burns, "18 Play-Along Facts about Shari Lewis and Lamb Chop," *Mental Floss*, June 9, 2016.

8. Veteran writers Elias Davis and David Pollack wrote her nightclub act.

I was 'baby blue.' I'm never vulgar. But when you're in Atlantic City, in that circumstance—actually, now Vegas and Atlantic City have gone so family that I wouldn't even do that."

In addition to Las Vegas and Atlantic City, she appeared in casinos in Hong Kong and Australia. Wherever she went, Lamb Chop followed. Although her puppet's precocity raised eyebrows, it also restored Shari's recognition among adult audiences who had known her in the 1960s, when they were children. They had grown up together. They knew and loved each other. Now was the time to use it.

10

Building a Business

Rejuvenated in the late 1980s under the corporate banner of Shari Lewis Enterprises, Shari began to flourish anew. Though others might have found it noteworthy that a woman was running her own multimedia company at a time when studios and networks relegated women to low-level "development" jobs, for Shari it was simply business as usual.

The first floor of the Tarcher house was reserved for family and meetings. Georgia Anderson was the chief cook and majordomo; she was later assisted by a woman named Teresa during the last decade of Shari's life. The bedrooms and business offices were on the second floor, where a staff of five fielded Shari's orders: Todd Tillson and Gordon Lamb were her drivers, Robert Kernan was her office manager, and Judy Wexler, A. J. Trotter, and Richard Seymour handled clerical duties and follow-through. Her manager, Jim Golden, scouted for work. Official office hours were weekdays from nine to six (except for special appearances), but Shari operated on Shari-time. She would dictate orders into a microcassette recorder and leave the tiny tapes on the appropriate person's desk for

"First thing for sure, when you hear my voice, without fail. . . ." That instruction was on just about every action item. And everything was an action item—do this, do that, make an appointment, get the alterations person in, schedule Nancy, the woman who did her eyelashes (applied one by one). We would laugh and then do it. "Honey, first thing for sure when you hear my voice, without fail, call so-and-so or set up so-and-so or buy such-and-such." When I heard the instructions I'd drop everything and do it. Whoever heard it would implement it.

—*Judy Wexler*

attention the next morning. At midday, Georgia served everyone lunch. This was not always a good thing, recalls Wexler, who began working for Shari in 1992. "It was presented to me when I first got the job that Georgia is the cook and she will feed you a beautiful lunch and we all eat together. That was cool. And then as the years went by I felt like we were prisoners at lunch and Georgia's making things that I really don't like. But it was an interesting dynamic."

"When I came in in 1993," says Seymour. "I wasn't really familiar with her work. I got to know that as I worked for her. But it wasn't until I saw her perform live at Magic Mountain, which was local, and I saw her onstage, I realized why she was a star. She had that magnetism, that charisma about her. She just drew you into her immediately." It was the same, he discovered, around the office. "You could just be in the room with her across from the table, not even with the puppet on her hand, just her hand, not anything on it, and you could believe her, that her hand was talking. She could make you believe that that thing she had on her hand was an entity separate from herself—a pretty genius thing to be able to do."

It was around this time that writer Sonny Gordon entered Shari's sphere. A gagman with eclectic TV credits, he was an expert at inventing special material and, like others in his field, sold his jokes for *X* dollars apiece. "It wasn't that she wanted another writer or wasn't pleased with any of the writers that she had," Gordon says, "it's just that somebody called her up through somebody she knew, so it validated that I was at least someone who knew someone that she knew. That's how that started. I don't know how she kept her spirits up," Gordon marveled, "but I know that the one thing she always, always loved was that she loved to laugh. No matter what kind of day she was having, when she heard something funny, it didn't have to go through any kind of filters, she just laughed."

"She was someone who had to be busy," agrees Susan Miller, who began handling Shari's merchandising in 1988 and visited the Tarcher-Lewis house on occasion. "It was filled with energy. It was the first time I had experienced people working at home in LA. In one corner you could hear a piano rehearsal; celebrities were in and out; upstairs there was a full-on office. Very busy and very scheduled and very focused but she always had time. There was always lunch there. She was a mom.

One night, a week before Christmas in 1994, I think, I got a mildly frantic phone call from Shari. She was getting ready to go out on a seasonal Christmas tour starting on the East Coast in Pittsburgh. She came up with an idea which was pretty cool. She said, "Why not make up a Christmas song introduction first, only make the first line of the actual song the punch line?" I spent the rest of the day trying to force it. Trying to force something makes you constipated right away. I fell asleep at the computer and woke up the next morning, and it occurred to me. I headed over to Shari and Jeremy's house at 8:30 a.m. Shari had her hair up in curlers and Jeremy was only half up. He had a "this better be good" look on his face. So I performed the verse, making up the melody:

> William Wally Chestnut was an anthropologist loved by all who labored at his side
> A strong believer in the rule of thumb but not the fist, he ventured every jungle far and wide
> Looking for the missing link to Man, the thing between the animal and Homo sapiens
> But William Wally Chestnut turned up missing one year full, Everyone who loved him filled with dread
> Until one day a colleague met a friendly cannibal
> And, when asked where William was, here is what the cannibal said:
> "Chestnut's roasting on an open fire. . . ."

Shari just burst out laughing. She pounded the table and she laughed—everything a joke writer wants to hear. She said she was putting it into the act immediately. Jeremy said, "Shari, can I see you?" They had a little office off to the side. Jeremy told her, "I don't think you should use it, it's a bad idea, it's gross for Lamb Chop." She told him she appreciated his opinion but she was going ahead and she used it anyway. The night she performed it, after the performance, she called me from Pittsburgh and told me it was the biggest laugh of the evening and thank you. Now, normally, back then, jokes went for fifty bucks, sometimes seventy-five, and less often a hundred. I received a check in the mail a couple of days later for five hundred dollars. That's the kind of lady she was.

—*Sonny Gordon*

People stayed with her a long time and everybody learned a great deal from her."

Todd Tillson worked most closely with Shari, rising over the years from driver to assistant to technical director, archivist, and a bit of everything else. A Seattle native, he had moved to Los Angeles with a friend who was working for Shari; then, when Shari fired the friend, Todd landed the job. One of the first things he noticed was how the public behaved around his new boss. "We would go to shows and people would be giddy to be close to a celebrity," he says. "They would approach me and ask, 'Is she really that sweet all the time?' and I would look at them and say, 'No, that would be sick. She's a human being, a high-profile human being, but she's everything that you or I are, except a little more electrified in some ways.' In many ways she was contradictions in terms and would try to play herself off as a regular person even though everyone, including herself, knew that wasn't the case."

> We were shopping at FedCo. We saw this woman who looked familiar, and I thought she was a friend of my mother. I said, "Excuse me, you look familiar to me." And she said, "I'm Shari Lewis." I said, "Oh my God, I grew up with you!" Now flash-forward a few months later. I was looking for a job. I got a call that was the most spaced-out call ever: "Um, hi, um, you answered an ad in the *Hollywood Reporter* for an assistant." When I heard the message I wasn't even sure I was going to call this person back because they sounded cuckoo to me. But I called back and said, "Who is this?" and she said, "It's Shari Lewis." I said, "Oh my God, I just saw you in FedCo!" So when I went to her house to interview I saw the mezuzah on the door and said, "Okay, I'm gonna get this job." Another Jewish girl from Beverly Hills. And that's exactly what happened.
>
> —*Judy Wexler*

While Shari's star was rising, so was Jeremy's, but in a separate universe. His New Age interests were taking hold among consumers, and his publishing partner, St. Martin's Press, was beginning to take his book sales more seriously. St. Martin's art director Deborah Daly had been dispatched to help Jeremy with his book covers, which, she said, quoting the publisher, "were terrible, which we all knew." According to Daly, "Jeremy thought in the beginning that I was a spy from St. Martin's (which, of course, I wasn't), but then I went on to be his freelance art director for twelve years." Once she was in Los Angeles, Daly was recruited by Shari in what had become her traditional manner. "I know Mallory," Daly continues, "and I have social things with Mallory, and then I'm doing business with Jeremy, and when I met Shari it was probably at a Christmas party or something like that. She said to me, 'Well, my daughter thinks you're wonderful and my husband thinks you're wonderful so I guess that means we will be working together in the future.' And I didn't know what to say." Daly quickly came to appreciate Shari's forthrightness and trust: "She knew exactly what she wanted, and what she didn't give you as information was the job she expected you to do for her."

Focusing on her career kept Shari busy and driven. Perhaps this was the impetus, or perhaps it was Jeremy's rising status as a major publisher of New Age works, but he began to spend personal time with one of his authors, Marilyn Ferguson. She had been divorced from her second husband, Michael Ferguson, since 1978 and was single. Jeremy was not. Her book, *The Aquarian Conspiracy: Personal and Social Transformation in the 1980s,* was zooming up the best-seller charts and became a major force in Tarcher Press's success. A bold yet nebulous statement of New Age positivity and the ability to make society better, it launched Ferguson, a humanistic psychologist and publisher of the *Brain/Mind Bulletin,* into full media mode. This, combined with her aura of fame, made her especially attractive, and soon she and Jeremy had launched too.

First, the backstory: Like Jeremy, America was primed for the New Age. "I published books I cared about rather than books that people thought would sell," he admitted to *Publishers Weekly* in 2013, "but it turned out that there were thousands of readers out there like me." The tide turned for him, he said, when he visited California's Esalen Institute, a nexus for New Age awakening.

Says Daly, "He hung out with those guys. He hung out with Nathaniel Branden and went up to Esalen and hung out at the Murphy [house] and those guys. That was the club. They were tossing that stuff around in their heads. They were his friends. Jeremy published stuff he was interested in. With Jeremy it was just kind of a wonderful exploration of Hilma af Klint,[1] a lot of artists I knew nothing about until I started doing his covers and hiring other people to do his covers as well."

Jeremy's publishing house had had a number of successful books, but he truly hit his stride with the New Age movement. It was all coming together. The "me" generation was starting to call itself "us" and was firing the cultural shots. Suddenly *lifestyle* was the buzzword for magazines, books, and TV talk shows. Thanks to Ferguson, Tarcher Press found itself at the forefront of a profitable psychic liberation movement. This bolstered Jeremy's self-worth in an age—make that New Age—when the Self was becoming all-important. Arguably, the affair with Ferguson also boosted his self-image.

Jeremy had been born Jewish but it quickly wore off; he considered himself not so much assimilated as lacking an identity. "Dad went to an ashram either before or after college," Mallory says. "He'd always been a lost boy easily swayed. He was a shitty student in school, dyslexic. My grandmother produced a son but didn't actually want one. She didn't like men. He fell into the whole New Age thing because it was the anti–work ethic. It was the anti-success. It was everything my mother hated, from the drugs to the promiscuity. And it was all bullshit."

Marilyn Ferguson was all that Shari was not, at least to Jeremy. "Dad was really into Esalen," Mallory recounts. "My parents' marriage broke when he started sleeping with Marilyn Ferguson, who was, to my mind, a raging piece of New Age crazy. He grew a beard and he told my mother that he was having an affair by taking her to Esalen and convincing her to take ecstasy.[2] Mom had no interest in drugs at all, but she was desperate to save her marriage. While at Esalen, after convincing her to take a hallucinogenic, he told her. When she was at her most vulnerable, he broke her heart."

Perhaps it was foolish for Jeremy to think that a confession would clear the slate, but wait: Shari Lewis took the mind-altering drug ecstasy?

1. Klint (1862–1944) was a Swedish abstract artist and mystic.

2. Ecstasy (3,4-methylenedioxymethamphetamine) is a recreational drug that produces enhanced pleasure, intimacy, and energy. Coming down from it, however, or using it repeatedly can lead to paranoia, vision problems, and rapid heartbeat.

"Once," Mallory confirms, expressing bitterness not toward her mother but toward her father. "I knew my dad was having an affair before I moved to college in 1980," she continues. "And I know how difficult the Marilyn years were for Mom, as they would be for any woman whose husband was cheating."

Nancy Sales, whose tenure with Jeremy overlapped Mary Lou Brady's, was there for the affair. "I had a feeling [Jeremy] was [seeing her] but I wasn't privy to it and I was still pretty young to think about things like that. [And I thought] Jeremy Tarcher wouldn't do things like that! I do remember one line during that period of time that I thought was pretty funny on that particular subject. Shari came back from a trip all excited because she was on a plane with Sean Connery and Michael Caine and Jeremy's reply was, 'Well, one's a fag and one's an old man,' and Shari's reply was, 'Darling, neither is a fag and you should be such an old man.'" Mallory, hearing this story, adds, "Mom told me that on that trip they made a massive play for her for a threesome because they were promoting *The Man Who Would Be King* and they were traveling around the country picking up girls, but when she turned them down they picked up the stewardess, who seemed rather happy as they left the plane together. I remember I was old enough to be told that story but young enough to think they were old, and I said, '*You turned them down*?'"

Sales worked closely with Jeremy during this period, which she describes as "painful. I just didn't want to believe it. I kind of always knew it, I just didn't want to believe it. All those people were so full of shit. Jeremy was in the forefront of New Age books. They were all talking about a wonderful life and believing in things, and yet they were the first ones to call up when they got the royalty statements. That was always such a turn-off to me. I actually thought most [New Age stuff] was absolute bullshit."

It was hard to reconcile New Age morality with marital vows and the goings-on between Ferguson and Jeremy. "I wouldn't believe it," Brady says. "I didn't want to. First of all, I thought she was a dog. But she was saying the things that he wanted to hear."

Ferguson remarried in 1983 to Ray Gottlieb. Their union lasted until 1991. Ferguson died in 2008 at age seventy and was celebrated as a "galvanizing influence" on her times. Jeremy released a statement saying that her book was "the Bible of the New Age" and that its once radical views had been accepted. He also credited her with his personal epiphany.

"I didn't really know about [the affair] until I came there one morning and found the foyer and stairs festooned with all of his wardrobe thrown all about," says Todd Tillson, who had only been working for Shari a short time. "I just walked into this cloud of 'what the hell's going on?' It was obviously placed there on his behalf, sort of like, 'Here's your shit.' He may have gone and stayed somewhere, a hotel, or maybe she was going out of town, whatever it was. That was the pall in the air for a while. I was just skirting around the edge of it, ignoring the obvious elephant in the room."

Shari got the last word: she mailed Ferguson a dead rat. Unlike a puppet, it didn't talk, but it sure did speak. Jeremy never saw Ferguson again.

Mom was aware that Dad was having an affair with Marilyn Ferguson. We lived in Beverly Hills. Beverly Hills has basements, and Beverly Hills has rats, and we had rat traps in the basement. Right after Mom confirmed Dad's affair, she asked Todd to go down to the basement and bring her a rat. She put it in a shoe box with a note that said, "This is what a woman who sleeps with another woman's husband becomes reincarnated as." Mom was not a fan of New Age reincarnation nonsense, and she certainly wasn't a fan of Marilyn—or the rat. As a postscript, she sent it third-class mail.

—*Mallory*

Compounding the rift at home, Shari's and Barbara's father died on September 19, 1981, at Doctors Hospital in Hollywood, Florida, at age seventy-four. Doc and Ann Hurwitz had moved to nearby Hallandale, Florida, seven years earlier, after his retirement from Yeshiva University. Shari never discussed the details of her father's passing, but Pat Brymer remembered going with her to a showing of *E.T. the Extraterrestrial* during a break from shooting in the summer of 1982. "She was fascinated with how it was done. We went to see it at the Cinerama Dome. We walked in and she was immediately mobbed by adults. The kids didn't know who the hell she was. We got into the theater and we got to the scene where ET was dying. All of a sudden she reached over and just grabbed my hand and she started squeezing it. Later she told me that she was squeezing the life out of my hand because it reminded her of her father's death."

Ann continued to live in Florida but made frequent trips to stay with Shari and Jeremy in Los Angeles. She would eventually move there permanently.

As always, Shari's way of deflecting personal hardship was through work. In 1983 she decided to carve out her own territory in the burgeoning new medium of home video. It would lead to another series—for which she is remembered by a whole new generation.

11

Video Days

Reinvention is both a motivation and a collaborative process. For a performer, it takes the cooperation of the media to demonstrate that, as the saying goes, "Everything old is new again." The average performing artist's popularity rarely spans more than one generation: the audience outgrows the artist, who fails to attract a new one. For every performer whose longevity makes him or her a legend (Bob Hope, Tony Bennett, Barbra Streisand, Peggy Lee), there are many more flashes in the pan. It's hard to make a comeback if you never were, so you might as well go into real estate (as many former celebrities do).

Even though Shari chafed at being thought of solely as a children's entertainer, she couldn't escape it. Thus, she had to face the reality that her primary audience was guaranteed to grow up. And yet she also had an advantage: her puppets were ageless, and together they had "raised" successive generations of kids who, by the 1980s, had ascended to positions of power in the television industry and were eager to put their own children into her hands, just as their parents had done with them. She exuded the same sense of assurance and security that made Fred Rogers and *Sesame Street* intergenerational favorites. All those former fans were now the grown-ups responsible for financing and booking programs, and Shari benefited from their affection.

"Friends and fans wonder what Shari and Lamb Chop will try next," enthused Mary A. Fischer in a May 23, 1983, *People* magazine profile extolling Shari's popularity "long before the Muppets and *Sesame Street.*" Fischer lists Shari's talents as "magician, dramatic actress, juggler, ventriloquist, chorus girl, and Girl Scout troop leader," as well as professional pianist, violinist, singer, recording artist, and the author of twenty-two children's books on subjects ranging from origami to fairy tales. "After all," she quotes Shari as saying, "I am an entertainer." Observes Mallory, "If Mom was still around she would be a social media influencer with millions of followers. She was the best at changing with the times." The publicity-rich article raised a key issue that Shari had been struggling with her entire career. Although others thought of her primarily as a ventriloquist and a children's entertainer, she didn't. Shari could do practically anything, and she did. But the ventriloquism was so impressive that it blinded people to her other talents.

Saul Turteltaub, her old friend from summer camp who later became one of her chief writers, also wrestled with the quintessence of "Shari." "She is a comedienne," he says. "She not only can deliver comedy well, she *enjoys* comedy. I mean, she'll read a script and if there's a good joke in there she'll laugh and laugh and laugh before she gets to the next line, and she'll want to do a joke. So it's got to be funny. And then she looks for the characters of the puppets. Lamb Chop has to be sweet and innocent. The comedy often is somebody just stepping out of character for a second, but the character should be there because she has to keep those characters different. Norm and Diane and all those people on *Cheers* had to be different people, and so Charlie Horse, Hush Puppy, and Lamb Chop have to be different, and she looks for that. Then she looks for an honesty in the piece. It, first of all, shouldn't be violent—there's moments when they bang their heads, but it's something that children would understand. It shouldn't be over their heads; she doesn't look for us to write jokes that the parents'll laugh at or some insider across the street or some William Morris agent will say, 'Wow, I get that one,' because you don't write like that for Shari, you write what children will understand. And you don't sell the kids short. The children understand a lot more than just balloons blowing up."

Like Shari, Mallory knows in her bones how Lamb Chop and her brothers talk, but few writers nail it the first time. "Lanny [Lan O'Kun] could write for the puppets," she says. "Other than Lanny, people would get close, but it either sounds right coming out of our mouths or it doesn't. Sometimes it's only a word or two, sometimes it's the difference of an attitude. We had really good writers on the show. Aubrey Tadman was a great writer for our show. It's not a matter of them doing it well or badly, it's a matter of any actress taking a line and making it her own. Lamb Chop is as much of an actress as she is her own person, as is Hush Puppy, as is Charlie Horse, as is Shari. They say it the way they say it."

Expanding on the concept that Lamb Chop is the princess, Hush Puppy is the middle child, and Charlie Horse is the big brother, Mallory says, "Lamb Chop was a six-year-old girl, the center of attention and the apple of her own and everyone's eye. Hush Puppy was an eight-year-old boy. He would get a bike and Lamb Chop would borrow it and Charlie Horse would convince Hush Puppy to buy the bike back from him. Charlie Horse was your classic brash older brother. He did have a heart of gold, but he would pick on his siblings, although if anyone else picked on Lamb Chop or Hush Puppy, he would beat 'em up."

The key detail that all of Shari's writers over the years needed to remember (because it reflected her own ethic) was not to talk down to children. "What Lan O'Kun and I did in those days when we were writing the show," says Turteltaub, "was that you wrote things that you thought they would understand and then you wrote as high up on that scale as you could go because you could teach them. It's amazing. I saw a little five-year-old kid the other day on the news singing opera in Italian. It was because he had liked that sound and learned it. Kids today at five years old are starting school knowing how to read and write. With me it didn't happen till I was in my second year of college. But the children today, not that they are smarter than they were years ago, they are more educated, they have been taught to learn more, and so they can learn so much more than people think they can. Unfortunately, they learn the bad, too. I mean, they see the shows that are violent and some of them do violent things. And I don't blame the writers of the show for anything; the parents raise the kids, the writers of the shows don't raise the parents' kids. So you write stuff that you can teach them and if you have something that they might not know, you *tell* them what it is. If you write about Columbus and they're not up to Columbus, you say who he is. And then you write your Columbus routine. This is not to put down adults, but the kind of laughs we used to get from children, the parents would watch and laugh, too."

In 1983 Shari received the John F. Kennedy Center Award for Excellence and Creativity. That same year she made her home video debut.

It was another reinvention for her, only this time she was using a new medium that was still in the process of inventing itself.

Video moved from television stations into people's homes in 1975, the year Sony debuted its Betamax video recorder and player. Two years later JVC (the Victor Company of Japan) introduced VHS,[1] which quickly overtook Betamax as the preferred format for personal video recording, playback, time-shifting, and program storage.[2]

Home video had a difficult birth. The earliest blank tapes cost upward of $25 apiece, and prerecorded tapes of the few movies that had been licensed for video cost as much as $99.95. Content was sometimes speeded up to fit longer films onto cassettes that then had a two-hour maximum length. Until a cheaper sell-through product was innovated (such as Disney's *Dumbo* and several of its less commercially successful features that sold for $26.95), the only ones who could afford to build a library of titles were video rental stores, which started popping up across America with the fecundity of 7–11s.

The field was ripe for the picking, so Shari got together with MGM/United Artists Home Entertainment in 1983 to produce and release *Have I Got a Story for You, You Can Do It,* and *Kooky Classics* at the affordable price of $29.95. Shari and MGM/UA knew something that only the Disney people had discovered: unlike adults, kids can watch TV shows a dozen times before they tire of them.[3]

As was her wont (and her father's mission), Shari combined entertainment and education in these videos. Rather than a six-minute stint on a variety show or guest appearance on someone else's series, these videos gave her nearly an hour to work with, allowing for even more polish than she had time for in her 1960s shows. She and her writers planned the home videos to be evergreens.

1. VHS stands for Video Home System.

2. Home video owes its early popularity to pornography, but that's another story.

3. In 1985 the Walt Disney Company was just about to release the first of its "crown jewels," *Pinocchio,* on home video. Jeffrey Katzenberg, then Disney's vice president of production, sagely remarked (in a conversation with the author) that he hoped home video wouldn't kill the film's theatrical reissue potential, but even if it did, the kids would wear out the tapes and have to buy another copy anyway. So either way, the company would come out ahead. *Pinocchio* sold 600,000 VHS units on its first release.

Shari Lewis dancing with Fred Gwynne. They met when Shari guest-starred on Gwynne's TV series *Car 54, Where Are You?* Fred returned the favor by playing Lamb Chop's doctor on *The Shari Lewis Show.* Of course, Lamb Chop developed a crush on him.

The Mount Rushmore of ventriloquists: Jimmy Nelson & Farfel; Mortimer Snerd, Edgar Bergen & Charlie McCarthy; Jay Johnson & Bob; and Shari Lewis & Lamb Chop with Steve Allen.

Mallory and Shari during production in Canada.

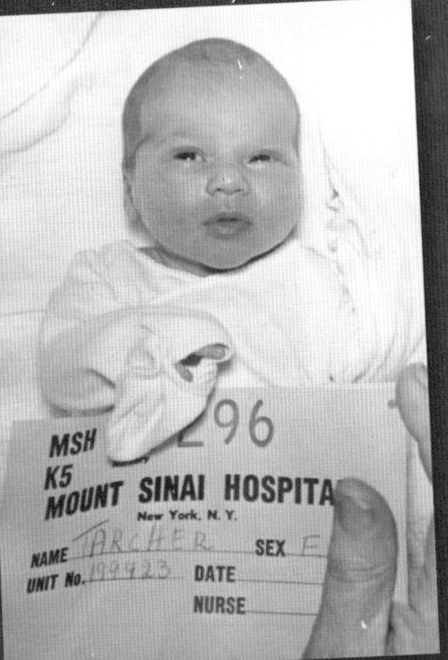

Mallory was born July 8, 1962—an event strategically planned to occur during summer hiatus so as not to interrupt Shari's TV schedule.

Mallory, Jeremy, and Shari Tarcher.

When she didn't have her hand in a puppet, Shari had it on a baton. Conducting orchestras was her second, no third, no fourth talent.

Shari surrounded by fan letters and one of her early puppets.

Barbara, Shari's younger sister, tries on hats. She became a dancer and a model and is now one of Los Angeles's most successful high-end decorators.

Abe "Doc" Hurwitz shows daughter Barbara a magic trick.

Shari and Samson, an early vent dummy that she retired in favor of Lamb Chop when Captain Kangaroo's producer advised her to get a softer puppet.

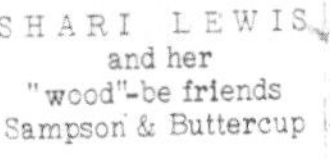

Shari, Samson, and Buttercup in a publicity montage sent to agents and bookers in the mid-1950s.

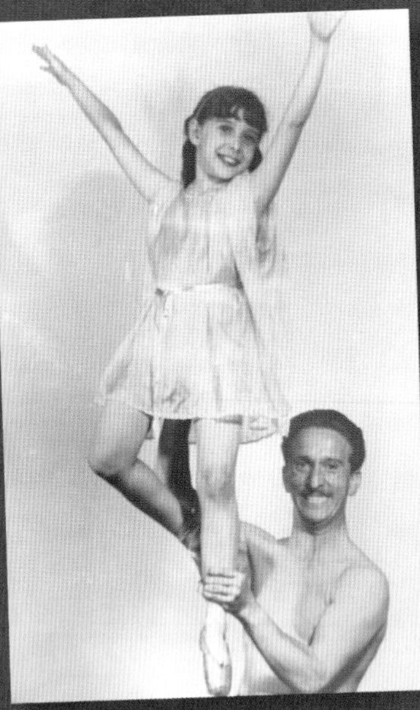

Abe hoists young Shari in the air as part of his act. Later she would do the same with Lamb Chop.

Shari took ballet lessons that paid off throughout her career.

N. Y. POST —
NOV. 22, 1951

Shari Hurwitz To Star In Young Israel Youth Variety Show Benifit

SHARI AND POPPET

Shari Hurwitz, talented daughter of "Peter Pan, the Magic Man," Dr. Abe Hurwitz, noted entertainer, will be featured in the program for the children's variety show to be presented on Sunday afternoon

Newspaper announcement for Shari and Buttercup's appearance at a charity show. Early exposure was crucial for her development as a performer. By this time, she had changed her name from Phyllis to Shari but was still Hurwitz.

Shari and Barbara perform a double act for the camera.

The Hurwitz family, early 1950s. Clockwise from left: Ann, Abe, Barbara, and Shari.

Ann, Shari (still Phyllis Naomi), and Abe, circa 1939 or 1940.

Shari is the baby sitting on her great-grandma's lap with her mom (left) and grandma (right).

Ann and Shari at Camp Shari, the source of her new first name.

Barbara Hurwitz at Camp Shari, probably 1946.

Shari blossomed at Camp Shari, late 1940s.

Shari, Abe, and Ann.

Mother and daughter show off their dual Emmy Awards. They won several.

John W. Cooper and his puppet, Sam Jackson. Cooper was a major influence on Shari when her father prevailed on him to teach her ventriloquy.

When not throwing her voice, Shari was using it to sing in a number of touring productions, including *Funny Girl*.

(*left*) Shari, her sister Barbara, and Barbara's husband Lan O'Kun. Lan was Shari's chief writer and songwriter as well as her brother-in-law.

(*below*) President Jimmy Carter kisses Shari at the White House. This was the second take. The camera didn't catch the first one, so Carter did it again. Lamb Chop's thoughts on the matter aren't known.

Contact sheet of Shari and Lamb Chop.

Jackie Cooper and Shari confer offstage.

(*bottom*) Dom DeLuise visits Shari and the gang on *The Shari Lewis Show.* Dom played a private detective named Kenny Ketchum (say it out loud), giving the beloved comic actor important early exposure.

Shari holds her own against one of the great comics, Morey Amsterdam.

The versatile character actor Hans Conried and Shari are ready to perform what looks like a circus act.

Shari and actor Robert Vaughn (as Napoleon Solo) between takes during her guest appearance on an episode ("The Off-Broadway Affair") of Vaughn's hit TV series *The Man from U.N.C.L.E.*

Shari appeared on *The Jack Benny Program* on March 18, 1962, which led to her performing with him in Las Vegas.

Shari cuts up with Steve Allen.

Shari and Jack Benny.

Shari with the gifted Burr Tillstrom and his hand puppets Kukla and Ollie. Fran (Allison) must have had the day off.

Shari and Jack Benny discuss the violin, an instrument they both played—differently.

Shari dances with two life-sized showgirl puppets, both of which are fastened to her. She had them made with chubby legs to make hers look thinner.

Shari sings with Robert Goulet as Lamb Chop swoons and Charlie Horse looks on.

Shari and Lamb Chop charm Dean Martin, who charmed them right back.

Shari and Danny Kaye as puppets. Shari appeared on Kaye's show twice.

Shari and the showgirls.

Shari, Samson, and a clutch of young fans. Samson may be reflecting Shari's state of mind at the encounter.

(*left*) Shari and Wing Ding, an early jazzy puppet. Wing Ding flew south and spent the rest of her days in Lan O'Kun's home office.

(*middle; left to right*) Shari with cousins Carol and Mel Hurwitz, sister Barbara, and cousin Ely Hurwitz.

(*bottom*) Shari with Lan and Barbara O'Kun.

Shari with Pat Morita.

Shari and Lamb Chop visited Africa and discovered that Lamb Chop was universal.

Having left the showgirls, Shari got "hitched" to an elegant, top-hatted dancing puppet who was not Fred Astaire. They were a hit onstage, and it was an adventure traveling with him on airplanes.

Shari and a very young Lamb Chop.

Shari and Lamb Chop in the middle years.

Shari and Lamb Chop back then and more recently. According to Mallory, you can tell the age of Shari's fans by what color they think her hair was.

Shari and Lamb Chop in the later years. How does Lamb Chop stay so young?

David McCallum, Shari, and Robert Vaughn do *The Man from U.N.C.L.E.*

Shari and Lamb Chop posing as *Playboy* bunnies.

Time to Go was an early edutainment show that Shari hosted. Much of her ear TV work was live and is now lost to time

Not one to miss a chance to entertain, Shari and her friends cut records. Over the years she issued many albums and videos telling stories and singing songs.

In those days, all young female performers were expected to do pinups, and Shari did not disappoint. Presumably Lamb Chop excused herself because she is easily sunburned.

Shari and comedienne Phyllis Diller. Most people don't know that Diller was a superbly trained concert pianist.

(*top*) Shari looking diaphanous.

(*middle*) Shari enjoys a bubble bath with a prop cigarette holder.

(*bottom*) Shari poses with a TV camera in the days of live TV. Compare this behemoth with the lipstick cameras of today, which produce better images.

(*top*) White gloves were de rigueur for any young lady in polite society in the 1950s. In most cases, Shari wore puppets on her hands instead.

(*middle*) Shari and Mr. Bearly greet their fans.

(*bottom*) Fans greet Shari at a book signing. Note the span of ages and her undiminished popularity.

Contact sheet for Lamb Chop where Shari is not present.

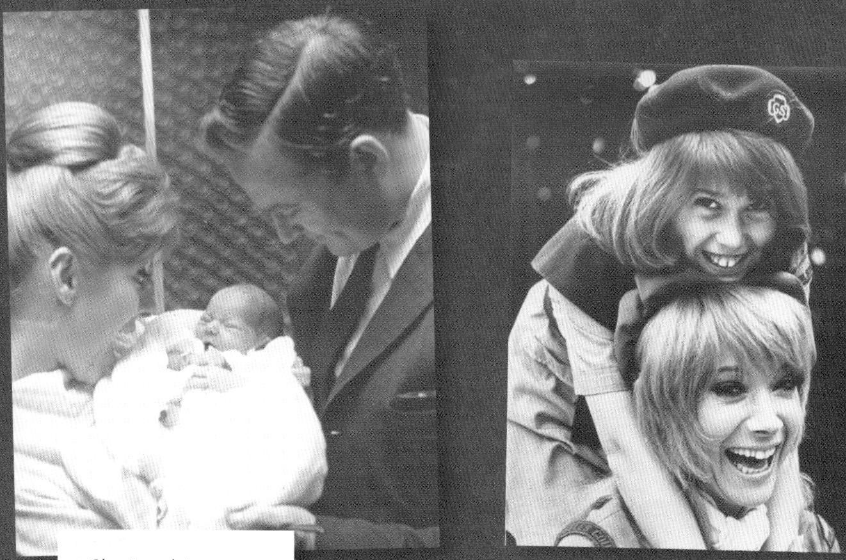

Shari and Jeremy hold newborn Mallory. (No, Shari didn't make the baby talk.)

Mallory in her Girl Scout uniform atop Shari. Neither had the heart to tell the other that scouting wasn't for her.

Shari and Mallory: partners, producers, family.

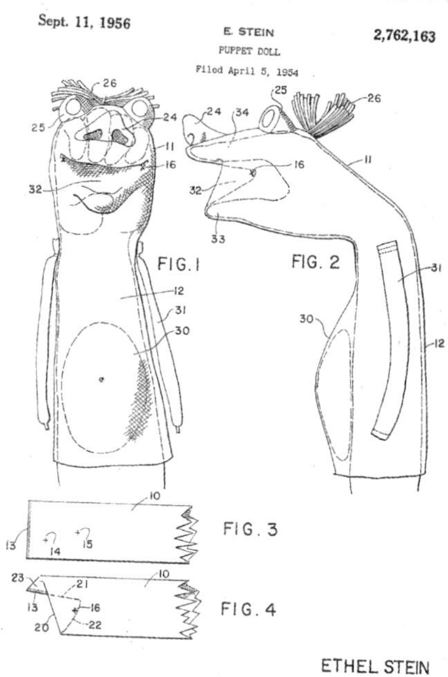

Diagram for an articulated puppet created by Ethel Stein. Stein's creation later became Lamb Chop. (Courtesy of Carl Stein)

Ethel Stein's early version of Lamb Chop prepares to go out into the world. (Courtesy of Carl Stein)

Mallory Lewis now performs with Lamb Chop and has done so since Shari's passing in 1998.

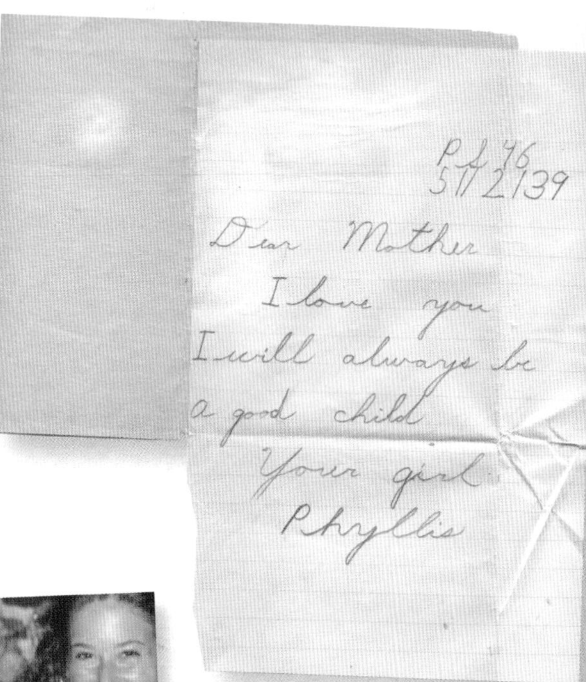

PS 46
5/12/39

Dear Mother
I love you
I will always be
a good child
Your girl
Phyllis

Shari—when she was still Phyllis—wrote a letter to her mother from PS 46 in the Bronx on May 12, 1939: "I love you. I will always be a good child. Your girl Phyllis."

Shari and Mallory, probably at a charity dinner.

Mallory's fifth birthday at a small amusement park in Beverly Hills.

(*middle*) Shari and Mallory cut loose in New Zealand. Jeremy said Mallory would never catch the lamb. He was wrong.

(*bottom*) Shari entertaining the troops.

Happy times for Shari, Jeremy, and Mallory in Martha's Vineyard.

(*left*) Shari and Jeremy in London in the 1970s.

(*bottom*) A letter from Shari to her beloved father.

To Daddy—

For tolerating my gener
nonsense.
For breaking me into the
ridiculous business.
For not minding my
minor league competit
For Bringing me up & let
me thing I brung
up m'self! —

Enjoy 'em—
Love,
Shari—
(alias Pinky,
Flea, Phyll)

Mallory and her amazing husband Brian Cummings.

Mallory and Brian Cummings at the Disney Lifetime Achievement Awards, where Mallory and Lamb Chop were recipients!

Mallory, son Jamie, and his daddy Brad at Tavern on the Green.

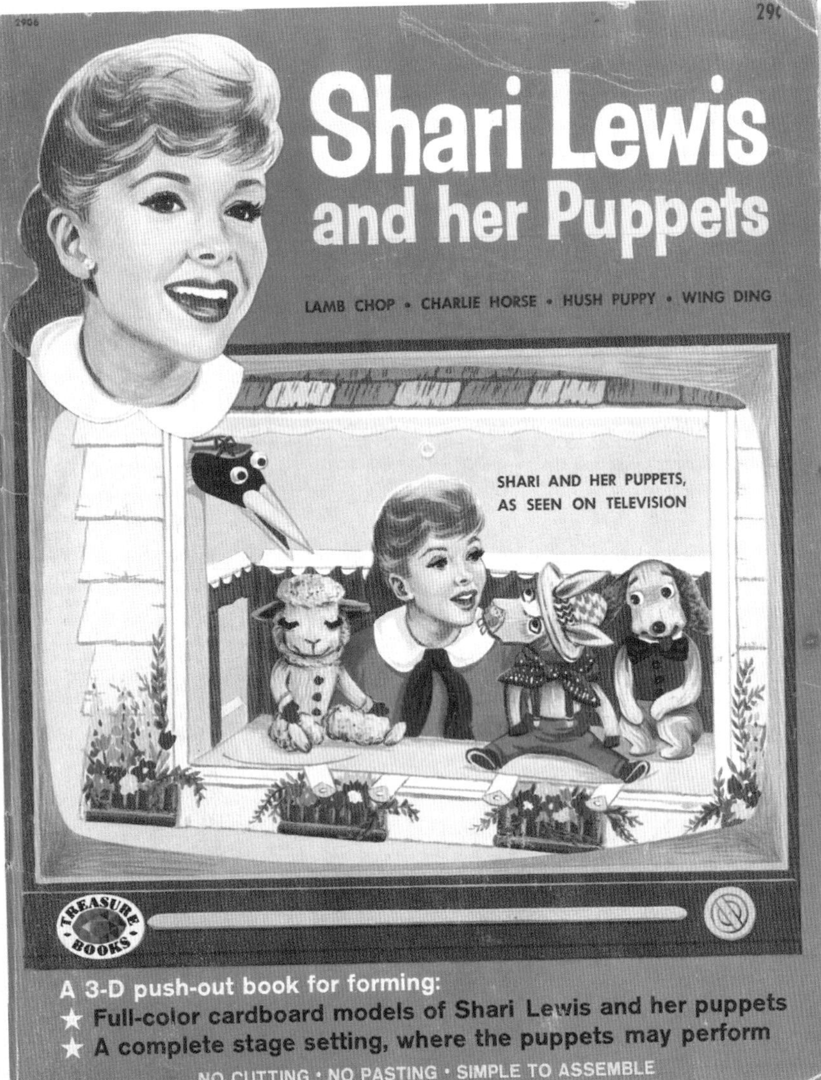

Shari Lewis and Her Puppets push-out book, 1961.

As before, the approach was key. Would she *teach* or would she *do*? "You can't force kids to like classical music," she cited as an example to Dennis Hunt of the *Los Angeles Times* when *Kooky Classics* was released.[4] "But if you introduce it to them in the right way, they may grow to like it. Make it fun, introduce children to the classics in a way that's fun for them. When they think of classics and classical melodies, they'll associate the music with fun, so they won't mind listening." She wasn't exactly Leonard Bernstein doing his *Young People's Concerts* (CBS, 1958–1972), but Bernstein was no ventriloquist either.

"Shari, who was always very multimedia, very cutting edge, always ahead of her time, had some concepts for some home videos," says Bernard Rothman, her producing partner in some of these ventures. "She sold them to MGM and asked me to be her writing partner (although the videos carry no writing credit) and produce them for her, and they were tough, but they're great and I'm happy to say they've lasted."

The home videos had solid production values. Directed and choreographed by Walter Painter, with songs by Norman Martin and Lan O'Kun, they featured people who would later become key contributors to Shari's TV series—notably, puppetry creative consultant Pat Brymer, creative consultant Stormy Sacks, and production assistant Todd Tillson,

Most of her earlier puppet masters left on bad terms. One disagreed with some of the things Shari wanted to do, saying they were impossible, so she got rid of him. When we were doing the dancing ladies (my first job for her), she made endless changes on them that would be to her benefit, so I did a lot of work—and you had to give Shari a contract price up front, a one-size-fits-all. Well, she took advantage of me, and when we got done and she had signed off on the dancing ladies, I said to her, "Just FYI, you've gotten a lot of free labor. In the future, if we keep adding and changing things, it's going to cost more money. I can't do it for a flat price." She said, "Oh, darling, you should have told me that before. I'll remember that. It will never happen again." And it didn't.

—*Pat Brymer*

4. "Shari Makes Classics Fun for Kids," *Los Angeles Times,* April 19, 1985.

who would be her all-around support person for nearly two decades. Brymer joined Shari's team after working for puppet mavens Sid and Marty Krofft and then for Hanna-Barbera in the latter's short-lived venture into puppetry. Shari recruited him in 1978, and he remained with her for the rest of her life—and even afterward. He also made Mallory's Lamb Chop puppets until his death. Lamb Chop and Mallory miss him greatly.

Although, technically, Lamb Chop is a sock puppet, there's more to her than that. "All the puppets were made on [Shari's] hand," Brymer discloses publicly for the first time. "She had very tiny hands; Mallory was the only other person who could fit into them. Building Lamb Chop for her was really tricky because she made all of those faces with her hand shape, so it had to be a perfect fit.[5] I would go over to her house every day when we were building Lamb Chop. She had a family room in the back where the piano was and a big table where we would have meetings. I would sit at the table on her right side"—he holds his arm up and cocks his hand ninety degrees—"and literally build Lamb Chop on her hand. I'd do the face and eyelashes and everything. She would put on a sweat sock. She had a special kind of sock that she used for Lamb Chop: Wigwam athletic wool sock.[6] We'd have to tuck and nip it and do all that stuff. She would approve the eyelashes, then we had to place the nose in a certain place, and she would approve that. I never saw her mouth move at all. You could be sitting right next to her making the Lamb Chop head and she could be writing with a pen with her left hand or doing business with someone at the table and she would turn her head to me and Lamb Chop would say, 'Well, how do I look now, Pat?' It was spooky. When the face was done, we would put the curls on the top. I would take it back to my shop and my assistant would build the arms and legs and assemble it all there. It turned out really well. I really

5. Shari would often rehearse while sitting in bed, her script laid out in front of her, moving her "naked" fingers without a puppet. Sometimes her fingers weren't the only naked thing. Todd Tillson remembers knocking on the bedroom door and Shari saying, "Come in," which he did, and saw her in the altogether. "She probably thought I was Jeremy," he later rationalized, "except why would Jeremy knock?"

6. The socks sell for $12.50 to $13.50 a pair. See www.wigwam.com.

streamlined Lamb Chop. I made her with longer legs and longer arms. She was pretty glam for a sock puppet."

Gary Hymowitz, who later coordinated the production of Lamb Chop plush toys for Golden Books (in addition to publishing and merchandising), was amazed at how complex the simple-looking sock puppet was. "Shari was so involved on the approval for the product," he says. "The plush, of course, was the key category for Lamb Chop. When it came to developing the actual puppet and reproducing the puppet, we had to bring the plush company up to Shari's house so they could sketch and photograph the original puppet because everybody thought it was going to be an easy puppet because it was just a white lamb, but they could never get the face right, the expression, the slant of the eyes, and the eyelashes. Everybody kept saying, 'This should be so easy; why is it difficult?' and Shari [kept] saying, 'It looks easy and it's not.' They came and actually did a pattern right from Shari's puppet in order to get it right."

Since Shari's passing, sadly, the estate lost control of product approval. "Shari would have been horrified by the dog toy that is currently in circulation," says Mallory. "It looks more like a camel than a lamb, and I really wish people would stop sending me pictures of their dog chewing on my little sister."

Susan Miller, whose Momentum Partners (now called Mixed Media Group) handled Shari's two-dimensional licensing (e.g., print, endorsements) in the late 1980s, experienced the same thing. "She wanted and completely trusted my team to make sure that whatever we did looked like Lamb Chop. The only thing that she would not do [was] . . . anything for kids that had sugar in it. She didn't want to do cookies or candy. She was very progressive; she felt it was just not good for kids. Of course, I wouldn't do anything that wasn't kid-appropriate, but that was the only 'no' for Shari." Although Shari had been writing books for years, it was Miller who brought Lamb Chop into publishing. "I did her first [Lamb Chop] book. She had never done Lamb Chop books, even though she'd been so successful earlier. In the nineties we did her first books and they were very successful."

Between writing books and making videos, it seemed that Shari didn't need broadcast television, but it was never far from her mind. TV fed her fame and conferred something that would later be called "brand identification." Over the next decade, she would create a full home library of "edutainment" titles, including *101 Things for Kids to Do* (1990) and *Don't Wake Your Mom!* (1992), leading up to the debut of the *Lamb Chop's Play-Along* television series in 1992.

What's noteworthy about this achievement is not just that Shari and her collaborators produced such a diverse and successful array of titles. The remarkable thing is that Shari did any of it at all: in 1984, at the age of fifty-one, she was diagnosed with breast cancer. It took ten years before she was able to discuss it with anyone outside of family and close associates. When she did, she spoke evenly, almost clinically, as though it had happened to someone else. "That is something that I handled well, resisting the doctors and functioning so that I knew what I wanted," she said calmly, once the worst was behind her. "It was handled beautifully and it's been ten years so I'm cool and it gave me a great sense of calm. It was probably the best thing that ever happened. It made me realize that you make yourself sick. You are one of the contributing factors to making yourself sick. Genetics played a big part. Therefore stress is simply to be avoided. I've never run away from it—I've tackled every job that needs to be done whether pleasant or unpleasant. But I don't feel stressful."

Instead, handling the stress fell to her daughter and husband. "It was very frightening when we found out that Mom had breast cancer," says Mallory. "She has always been indomitable." Adds Jeremy, "Shari dealt with her breast cancer in a quintessentially healthy manner, and one that is an example of the best of Shari Lewis."

She opted not to have a radical mastectomy. "I made my decision and then I was calm in pursuing the nonradical line that I pursued," she said long after she had recovered. "I really alienated a lot of our doctor friends. I did a Larry King [show] where I talked about the fact that particularly male doctors treat women as though they're babies, as though they're not equals, and that ticks me. I talked about it and women in the [studio] were shaking their heads yes, as we speak. It's very common and I think all that we can do is pleasantly remind the doctor of what he, or she, is doing when it happens, and then get another doctor."

Jeremy agreed. "A number of the doctors wanted to be much more radical in their approach than Shari chose to be," he explained, deferring to his wife. "That is not the way she would go about doing something, and so she didn't do it. Conceivably she could have been wrong—but she wasn't. Every doctor that she saw, she questioned with great care. She decided what was good for Shari and then pursued it with vigor. She put together essentially her own regime and followed it very carefully, and has had an extraordinarily good outcome." Nevertheless, under Jeremy's New Age influence, Shari augmented her medical treatment with holistic and herbal treatments. (What she could not have known at the time was that the medication she was prescribed—the powerful drug tamoxifen—would have disastrous consequences down the road.)

"It was not a nightmare," Shari concludes, putting her illness in perspective. "It was an experience because I was in control of it. And it's not that I'm a control freak—which may be the case, but it's not relevant to this, I think. Everybody should stay in control of their body and of what happens to it."

It was Mallory who had to adjust not only to her mother's illness but also to her attitude about it. "I would take her every day to the radiation [treatments]," she explains, "and then we would go to the Beverly Center and do a little shopping and make ourselves feel better. Until there was the day when we skipped radiation and just headed off to the Beverly Center. We were halfway through the second floor of Bullock's before we figured it out."

"And now, ten years later," Shari added in a statement that turned out to be sadly mistaken, "I'm fine—I'm poifect—and the course that we took obviously was the right course. So I feel very gratified by it." In truth, she was neither perfect nor poifect, only she didn't know it. The cancer would return. But so would Shari.

12

The Price of Fame

Fame is not normal. Despite Andy Warhol's annoying comment,[1] human beings are not meant to be recognized by strangers. The notion that somebody you don't know at all thinks they know you is the product of a civilization that has expanded beyond its tribal village origins. Originally defined as "being known and talked about for notable achievements," the meaning of *fame* has been corrupted, particularly since the rise of social media in the twentieth century. Today, a "celebrity" can be someone who is famous simply for being famous. Achievement is no longer required.

Shari, however, had achievements. Lots of them. The one nobody discussed—both because it was so unusual and because she designed it to function below the radar—was that she headed her own business. And it wasn't a simple D/B/A; it was a major enterprise. "Other than Lucille Ball," notes Mallory, "there were really no other women running their own entertainment companies at that time. The only thing that mattered to her was staying on the air, getting another TV show." And that took business sense. True, she had a manager in Jim Golden, a publicist in Maggie Begley, a musical director in Stormy Sacks, and a puppet master in Pat Brymer, as well as writers, accountants, lawyers, and a full office staff. But they all worked for her.

At the same time, by all accounts, she did not consider herself a symbol of the Women's Movement that was taking hold in the late 1960s

1. According to some sources, Warhol never actually said the words attributed to him: "In the future, everyone will be world-famous for fifteen minutes." Apparently, when onlookers interrupted a portrait session with Warhol, it was photographer Nat Finkelstein who said, "Everyone wants to be famous." The artist then replied, "Yes, for about fifteen minutes," which, depending on the inflection, can have the opposite meaning.

(but had actually begun with the suffrage movement in 1848). To Shari, being in charge of her own life was a simple matter of doing what she had to do to achieve her goals. Whether she thirsted for fame per se or accepted it as a by-product of the joy she got from performing is a mystery that may never be solved. But she was famous, and there is no question that she handled it honorably.

Shari Lewis made her way in fields dominated by men—both ventriloquism and television. She perfected a talent that was not only a specialty but a niche, an oddity, a footnote in show business. And by the sheer force of her determination and talent, she turned it into an industry called Shari Lewis Enterprises. This drive made her difficult to work with at times, but even those who felt the sting of her demands admit that it was all in the service of her craft, not her ego. Her presence and her persona influenced three generations of both women and men.

Judy Wexler, who was also a jazz musician while she worked for Shari, was being interviewed about her new CD. "After the interviewer asked me about my musical influences, she said, 'I'm curious to know where you got your entrepreneurial inspirations.'" Wexler recalled, "I would usually think of my dad, who started a business and retired at fifty. But in that moment, I thought, you know what, it never occurred to me but I just had this thought, one of the main influences of my entrepreneurship is Shari Lewis. Because she knew what she wanted and was able to get it done. She rallied the right people around her. She got the job done."

"She was so talented," says an admiring Margaret Loesch. "Symphony conducting? Magic? Dancing? I was so impressed when I met with her in the 1990s. I'll never forget this; she was on her way to Japan to conduct a national orchestra. We spent forty-five minutes talking about it. Every time I met with Shari I learned something else about her. She was an amazing woman." Loesch says of Muppet innovator Jim Henson: "He was very respectful of her, too. He talked about her as a talent because he thought that she had done a great job, and he made the comment—I can't remember the context—it was a flattering remark. He said something like, 'She's a one-woman band.'"

Says Jay Johnson, "She was always classy. With ventriloquists you can't always say that about them. They may be good and they may be great and they may be talented, but the person they are is eventually how you judge somebody. And Shari was, yes, a dynamo and, yes, a female that didn't want to be categorized as a secretary. She was very strong. But classy. She was never in a fight with anybody that I heard of, she was never at odds with the ventriloquist community."

Johnson agrees that she blazed her own trail as both a performer and a businesswoman. "She did what she needed to do. There wasn't an agenda there, it was just, 'I am a creative person, this is what we need to get done. If that's what I need to do at this moment, then I am going to do it.' She wasn't limited by any of that, and I think it came through to guys like me that were really just a fan for such a long time, to get to see that."

Shari was devoted to her fans. One who developed a privileged relationship with her was Heidi Hubbs. Hubbs was in her midteens when she first saw *The Shari Show*. "I think I was more fascinated with her than I was with the puppets," Hubbs recalls, "although who doesn't like Lamb Chop? A neighbor had gotten tickets for a ventriloquist show that was being filmed for a TV special over at Knott's Berry Farm. They knew I liked Shari Lewis, and that's the first time I got to see her live." Later, a friend of Heidi's worked at Disneyland, where Shari was making an appearance, and connected them. "I brought my little scrapbook," Hubbs continues, "and went to the stage door and they allowed me backstage. I was so excited. Had my picture taken with her."

Hubbs continued to meet Shari at live appearances, often bringing her mother along ("I think Shari kinda liked my mom because every time I would show up without her, she was, 'Why isn't your mom here?'"). Heidi amassed an inventory of signed books, posters, toys, and other

---

She was part mother, part inspiration, definitely boss, but when you worked for her, you could be totally yourself. She had a lot of characters surrounding her—comedy writers, songwriters, puppet makers—it was a cuckoo house. But they were all friends. I have this one memory when Milton Berle phoned and she was downstairs rehearsing. I said, "Oh my God, it's Milton Berle. Shari! It's Uncle Miltie! He's on line one!" And she was like, "Honey, I'm in a rehearsal. I'll call him back."

—*Judy Wexler*

---

merchandise. Shari appreciated her devotion. "I feel that she welcomed me with open arms," Hubbs says. "From what I've heard she didn't do that to many people, so I feel very fortunate. I wasn't some crazy fan. I noticed, too, that when she would meet people, she was cordial, but you could tell she kept her distance. When people tried to say things or get close to her, she'd kinda turn her head at me and roll her eyes. This made me feel a little more special that I was kind of in her inner sanctum."

On one special occasion, Shari even visited the Hubbs house. "She did an opening at a child-care center for United Health Care," Hubbs recalls. "After the appearance I said, 'You haven't seen my whole collection, and I live three miles from here.' She asked the limo driver to make a stop and came to my house and saw my whole collection. Let me tell you, I was on cloud nine that day!"

Mallory says, "One thing I remember is that my mom would always take my call. She'd interrupt any meeting if I called and say, 'Hi darling, are you okay? I'm in a meeting. Can I call you back or do you need me now?' She always took my dad's and my calls."

"She loved to shock people because she loved people's reactions," says licensing expert Gary Hymowitz. "In a restaurant one night, we had the center table so everybody could see her, and you could tell everybody was whispering, 'Look, there's Shari Lewis, there's Shari Lewis.' The waiter came over and asked her what she would like for dinner and very loudly she said, 'I'll have the lamb.' She loved that shock value."

Gary H. Grossman related a similar dining experience. Grossman and his wife, Helene Seifer, "went out to dinner with Shari and Jeremy and she would order lamb chops. I suddenly felt very uncomfortable. Where I come from we really don't eat our young. I think she liked lamb chops, but I think she also did that for effect." Susan Miller's dining experiences with Shari were even more grotesque: "Shari loved corned beef hash, but when we'd go out, she liked to order lamb chops to see people's reactions. Then she would tell the waiter as he walked away, 'And don't forget the mint jelly!'"

Although she didn't socialize with fellow ventriloquists, Shari found time to mentor one. Like most kids, Carla Rhodes first saw Shari on television, got hooked on ventriloquy by reading a book,[2] and practiced on her own with a merchandised Lamb Chop puppet. "I carried her on the bus with me," Rhodes says. "You can get away with that when you're nine or ten years old. The coolest thing for me was that I had started writing her letters at least once a month, if not more. The letters would be like, 'Hi Shari, I'm Carla, I'm ten years old. This is what I've done in school this week. I want to be a ventriloquist. I want to be an artist.' She would encourage my art. She would always write little things in the margins. It was pretty amazing; I just couldn't believe that she would write back."

Carla and Shari finally met backstage in 1996 after one of Shari's performances in Cincinnati, not too far from Kentucky, where Carla was raised. "I showed her a hard dummy I'd made, and by then I think I was fourteen or fifteen years old. I remember her picking up this dummy and saying, 'I haven't held a figure like this since I did something with Paul Winchell in '63.' That was particularly amazing. She took me back to her trailer and gave me all this really great showbiz advice and was so kind to me."

Today Carla Rhodes is a professional ventriloquist whose primary puppet is Cecil, an abrasive talent agent. Shari helped Rhodes the way John W. Cooper, Monsieur Brunard, and Stanley Burns helped her. "Shari Lewis, without a doubt, had the biggest impact on my life," Rhodes says proudly. "Seeing her on TV inspired me to become a ventriloquist. She was a ventriloquist, she conducted orchestras, she wrote books. I got really great encouragement from her. It made me realize that dreams are really possible. I come from a broken home, and when she came into my life, in watching her on television, I felt like I had a friend." Carla Rhodes is also a hugely successful and much lauded wildlife conservation photographer and can be found on Instagram at @MissCarlaRhodes.

Offers Jay Johnson, "I was a big Captain Kangaroo fan and she was on *Captain Kangaroo.* Everybody had a crush on Shari. She could dance and she could sing and she was cute and had these great puppets, so I think it wasn't hard for all of us of an age to be in love with Shari Lewis. We had met each other a couple of times, passing at a party or something,

2. Alexander von Rensselaer, *Fun with Ventriloquism* (Garden City, NJ: Garden City Books, 1955).

but there was an HBO show called *The Vent Event.*[3] I remember doing 'Figaro' (from *The Barber of Seville*), which was my thing, and afterwards, Shari came over to me. She was really sweet, we took pictures and all, and she said, 'I didn't know you were going to do "Figaro."[4] I'm so glad that I didn't do [it].' My version wasn't her version. We all look for those rapid-fire songs, and we got to be good friends because we kinda dodged a bullet; nobody had to cut anything."

Mom was always a *huge* Jay Johnson fan. She thought he was an amazing actor as well as an amazing "vent" with his character Bob. She didn't have much to say one way or the other about most vents, but I always thought she and Lamb Chop had a crush on Jay and Bob.

—*Mallory*

Johnson had another memorable exchange with Shari while talking shop. "Once I ran into her on an airplane. We talked as we were traveling, and I said, 'Where's Lammie?' She said, 'Up here.' Lammie was in the overhead compartment in a Tupperware. I said, 'Lamb Chop travels in Tupperware?' She said, 'It's the safest thing I can do and it's easy.'"

There was, understandably, the occasional downside to Shari's celebrity; after all, the word *fan* is short for *fanatic.* One particular annoyance has plagued Mallory since taking up her mother's creation and gaining a public profile. "There's this person out there who claims to be my long-lost brother," she says. "I don't have a brother. Or a sister. I am an only child. But somehow the facts have not deterred him. I told him that he should spit in a cup and send it to 23 and Me and that I would be thrilled to find a new relative. Oddly, I haven't heard anything from him since."

Faux siblings notwithstanding, both Mallory and Shari learned early on to deal with the emotional effect Lamb Chop has on the public and even on celebrities who ought to be inured to fame. According to Mallory,

3. *The Vent Event* aired March 3, 1978, hosted by Steve Allen and with appearances by Shari Lewis, Jay Johnson, Edgar Bergen, Jimmy Nelson, Willy Tyler, and Lou Dupont.

4. "Figaro" is the famous tongue-twisting aria from Gioacchino Rossini's and Cesare Sterbini's opera *The Barber of Seville.*

"Celebrities get jazzed when they meet Lamb Chop. Chubby Checker said, 'Excuse me, I'm Chubby Checker, would it be possible for me to have a picture with Lamb Chop?' I'm like, 'Yes, that's not a problem.' Chubby fucking Checker! Ben Vereen and Fran Lebowitz were charmed to meet Lamb Chop. Even Betty White was a fan."

Some people were fine working with Shari but got freaked out by Lamb Chop. "Other performers [didn't grasp the concept of] working with a puppet," says Mary Lou Brady. "Some did it so naturally and would talk directly to Lamb Chop, but there were others that couldn't do it. Shari was on the Carson show with [opera singer] Jan Peerce and Lamb Chop started to talk to him and he couldn't do it. He kept looking at Shari, and Lamb Chop had to keep saying, 'No, no, talk to *me.*'"

Even presidents were not immune to Shari's charms. She made five appearances at the White House, but her most memorable was the time Jimmy Carter kissed her—twice. "That was a really funny story," Shari said. "What happened was, I walked in and he said, 'My daughter and I watch your show all the time,' and he gave me a big hug and a kiss. And I said, 'This is awful; here I am, I'm seated with forty photographers in front of me, and nobody took that picture. I'm gonna go home and tell my husband the president kissed me and there's no evidence.' And he said, 'Cameras to the ready.' And that picture was the second kiss. It happened fast, at the very beginning of the meeting. When I met Reagan for the first time, I was at the end of a reception line because I had been performing and everybody else had come out, and I had to get out of my clown costume. As I'm on the line, a lot of his young people in gray uniforms with white gloves are running up and whispering. When I got

When Shari traveled, Lamb Chop—like Mary's little lamb—was never far behind. It never went in Shari's luggage, just in case, God forbid, the luggage should disappear. It always went with her on the plane. When I traveled with her when we were launching *Charlie Horse Music Pizza*, we had to go to the PBS broadcasters' presentation, and I flew with her from LA to Dallas. The puppet had to be with her. It had its own little special case and plastic bag. She always protected that.

—*Gary Hymowitz*

up to him—he's quite tall, although by me everybody is tall—he looked down and he said, 'I certainly hope you have a sense of humor. I've been told to say that I watched you when I was a little boy.'"

With Lamb Chop speaking her unfiltered mind, Shari could relax. This led to a bizarre event related by Jay Johnson, as told to him by McLean Stevenson. Shari was a guest on the *Smothers Brothers Comedy Hour,* where Stevenson was a writer at the time (he later played Colonel Henry Blake on TV's *M*A*S*H*). He accidentally sat on Lamb Chop during a run-through after Shari had parked the puppet in one of the empty audience seats. The producer ordered Stevenson to apologize. According to Johnson, "McLean knocked on the [dressing room] door and Shari's at her makeup table. McLean says, 'Miss Lewis, I'm so sorry, I had no idea, I just reached behind and tossed it. I really wasn't aware. I'm so sorry. Please don't leave the show. We love you.' And Shari was really, really gracious: 'These things happen, McLean, I appreciate your coming in.' He's thinking, 'Wow, that went well,' and he turns. Now Lamb Chop is on her hand and he hears, 'What about *me*?' And he says, 'I got redressed by a sock! It was trembling in my face. I didn't know what to do, I didn't know what to say. I just stood there and was redressed by a sock!' I love that story. He loved to say he was humiliated by a sock. The fact that he told me the story with such affability and fondness let me know that it was just one of those great stories."

Shari's other characters have theirs as well. "She was appearing at the KCET store and she didn't have her puppets there," says Heidi Hubbs. "One little boy, however, brought her a bouquet of carrots to give to Charlie Horse."

"You want to know what Shari's like as an individual?" Steve Krantz asks rhetorically. "She's what, five foot one, five foot two; she's diminutive.[5] And, on the other hand, she has the energy sufficient to light up Baghdad if we ever bomb it again. She's really remarkable. But one of the other things that she does, which is important to watching her work and watching her, is that, as a woman, she is enormously appreciative of good work. She's very demanding, but the demands she makes of others are precisely the demands she makes of herself."

5. Says Mallory, "Actually, she topped out at five feet."

Susan Miller, who handled Shari's product licensing, agrees: "She was the best client I ever had—the most open-minded, clear, hardworking. She would call up and say, 'Hey, Susan, darling, I'm going to Dallas for my cousin's wedding. Who do you want me to meet with there? Is there an editor? Is there a TV station? A store buyer?' I learned from her, she was a mentor, I admire her. A rare breed."

"She had a lot of compassion," says Pat Brymer. "I remember when my mother died I was in St. Louis doing a video shoot for another company and I had to stay there and put things together. My sister was also there. I remember one morning the phone rang. I picked it up and it was Shari calling from LA. She had heard that my mother had passed. She had met my mother when my mother came out to visit and Shari invited her to breakfast. My mother was [starstruck]! She remembered my mother and how close I was to my mom and so she called me and told me how sorry she was." He pauses, moved. "She did have a lot of compassion." Then he adds, "She didn't show it too often."

"Shari appeals to the public," explains Saul Turteltaub. "She is talented and good at doing what she does. I don't know how they all look at her. I just know that parents like her and kids like her. Kids can like an adult without thinking of them as parents, so it's not necessarily material. Sometimes kids like her because she's not their mother, I would guess. I think men like her because she's cute to look at and she's talented and she may be sexy."

But perhaps the best words on her appeal, her fame, and the pressures that come with it are from Shari herself: "I just have come to realize that nothing good comes out of inner turmoil unless you have to make changes in your life, and then you have to respond to that. So the window-washer washed my window and scratched it. You deal with it, you don't get *shpilkes* over it." Continues Mallory, "As my mother used to say, stop taking your emotional temperature and move on."

13

Renaissance

Flashback: When the 101st Congress passed the Children's Television Act of 1990, there was hope that parents and children might gain control over the glass eye that had held young people in its thrall since the late 1940s. Among its provisions were that TV stations had to limit advertising in children's shows to no more than ten and a half minutes per hour on weekends and no more than twelve minutes per hour on weekdays;[1] establish a National Endowment for Children's Television; and admit that, in terms of education, children in the United States lagged behind those in other countries. The rest of the law was concerned with procedural matters, except for one notation: after January 1, 1993—three years hence—the FCC would examine how the new law was faring. In one sense, it was assessing the legacy of the deregulation-happy Reagan FCC that had bent to the desires of the TV industry. In another sense, though, it was showing the effect of that legacy.

Testifying before the House Telecommunications Subcommittee in support of the bill, Shari brought along a friend: Lamb Chop.

> Shari: May Lamb Chop just say a word?
> FCC commissioner: Of course, of course. Why didn't you say so?
> Lamb Chop: She did say so. [To Shari:] Where are we?
> Shari: We're at the FCC.
> Lamb Chop: How come you're nervous?
> Shari: I'm not nervous.
> Lamb Chop: Yes, you're nervous.
> Shari: How can you tell I'm nervous?

1. By way of comparison, in its heyday, prime-time adult fare had a limit of eight minutes of advertising per hour.

Lamb Chop: Your palm is sweaty.
Shari (examining her left hand): My palm is not sweaty.
Lamb Chop: No, the other hand.
Shari: What would you like to say?
Lamb Chop: Oh, oh, I would like to applaud the FCC for caring about children's television and making it better.
Shari: I would like to applaud the FCC too.
Lamb Chop: No, no, no! Let me do the applauding.
Shari: Why?
Lamb Chop: Cuz every time you clap your hands together, I black out.

Action for Children's Television founder Peggy Charren was at the hearings. "It was the most breathtaking piece of testimony I have ever heard in twenty-five years of running back and forth to Washington," she says. "She charmed the room, which works like a courtroom. When she held up Lamb Chop on her arm, Lamb Chop turned to Ed Markey, chairman of the House Telecommunications Subcommittee, and Lamb Chop said, 'Do I just get the rest of Shari's time, or can I have my own time?' And Ed Markey, the superhero of kids' TV, looked at her and said, 'You have all the time you need, Lamb Chop.' The whole room applauded. It was just the most wonderful time to be in a place where children's television was getting defended by someone who knew what she was talking about."

Later, in remarks for the record, Markey said, "Shari Lewis . . . pointed up her program as an example of a successful and profitable children's programming that not only entertained but also educated, and I suppose . . . that is one of my concerns as we address this issue." Markey went on to call for a balance between serving the children in the audience and recognizing commercial broadcasters' need to make money. He cautioned against allowing the government to decide on the quality of programing and urged "a fine mix, a fine balance, in television for children" that, "as Shari Lewis pointed out," would "be both successful and even profitable to the commercial broadcaster."[2]

Markey and Shari were talking, but for the longest time, nobody was listening. Jeremy, who watched her during those years, said that Shari

2. Edward Markey, "Children's Television (Part 2)," Hearings before the Subcommittee on Telecommunications and Finance of the Committee on Energy and Commerce, House of Representatives, 103rd Congress, 2nd session, June 10, 1994.

never let go of her vision. "She integrates a lot of her childhood wisdom such as Abe's maxims: 'The day begins the night before.' She is ready to start each day because she has, indeed, prepared herself for the next day in every way that she knows how. 'Have faith and be of good courage.' Shari has kept her sense of faith in herself and courageousness, particularly during a slow period—twenty years from the early sixties to the late eighties during which each year she kept producing that product, which is herself, until PBS was there to put her back on the air in 1991."

> Ventriloquy goes in and out of popularity. Go back to vaudeville, and it was a mainstay. Then you've got Ed Sullivan, who loved ventriloquists; Ricky Lane was on *The Ed Sullivan Show* forty-seven times, Señor Wences, Jimmy Nelson, and Edgar Bergen. When that went off the air, it bottomed out for a little bit because the masses weren't seeing ventriloquists as much. But you still had Shari and Willie Tyler and other of their contemporaries in the mid-1970s until you get to Jay Johnson on *Soap*. You don't see a lot in the 1980s because of the sitcoms dominating the world. But once *America's Got Talent* came on the air . . . you've got variety again, and three ventriloquists have won that show.
>
> —*Lisa Sweazy*

That was the year Shari proved once again that she was the queen of television with the creation of *Lamb Chop's Play-Along*. Just about to hit sixty, and having been a performer for nearly all that time, she turned her energies to reaching yet another generation. Said Stormy Sacks, her creative and musical consultant, "I think it was our first or second job together, and I said to her, 'What is your goal in this business?' And she said, 'Survival.' And she has more than survived. She has had this renaissance that is quite magical and quite wonderful."[3]

Play-Along marked Shari's return to network television after twenty-seven years. Conceived as a showcase for diversity (its human stars represented an ethnic mix), the series stressed social situations young viewers

3. Stormy Sacks, interviewed in 1994.

might find themselves in and showed the kids how to deal with them. It was the perfect forum for Shari.

"I think PBS has done a great job," says Margaret Loesch, who specialized in children's programming for commercial networks. "Now, you have to put it into some context. Yes, it's not ratings based, and the only way that programmers like myself [on commercial TV] could justify retaining shows or buying them was the expectation that they would deliver ratings. PBS was appropriately protected from ratings. Now, having said that, PBS was also very competitive in buying shows. It's just as hard to get a show on PBS, if not harder, than it is to get it on American network television. Back in Shari's time in the fifties and sixties, when she was doing shows for PBS, they paid for them. But that's been discontinued. To get a show on the air today on PBS, you have to go out and raise your money. It's very challenging."

Because PBS budgets were limited, Shari's production had to be well organized and intense. All the scripts for *Lamb Chop's Play-Along* were written before production began, scenes were blocked on paper, and segments were ganged up so they could be taped separately and combined into various episodes in postproduction. Although Shari lived in Los Angeles, the show was shot largely in Vancouver, British Columbia, which meant that the crew had to be 75 percent Canadian for Canadian tax credit purposes. (A few scenes were shot in Los Angeles in a mock-up of the Vancouver set.) Each episode took around two days to shoot, but that's just an estimate because the pieces were spread out over an entire production schedule and assembled later during editing.

Says Shawn Williamson, who was the show's associate producer (his Brightlight Pictures is now one of Canada's most successful and prolific production companies), "Now that I have a much deeper background in film and television, I realize that it was a tiny show, but to me it seemed huge, coming out of theater. It was typically multicamera, so we shot three cameras recording on tape, each camera iso'd, which means recorded on its own, and then the director would do a line cut, which was effectively a soft edit of what he or she would think the show might look like prior to air. With puppets, everything was on risers to give the puppeteers space to work underneath. They had rigging underneath, rods would come up, and wires and cables; hands and bodies would come up from underneath."

In Canada, we stayed at a hotel on Robson Street. It was a ten-block walk from the hotel to the CBC. It was one of the best shopping streets in the world, and we were getting per diems, and the Canadian dollar was worth nothing. Luckily, we were at the studio at seven o'clock and we left at six, so there was very little [time for shopping]. It's very interesting. When Mom died, I found her *knipple,* which is a Jewish word for the money a mom stashes away. And half of it was in Canadian dollars.

—*Mallory*

"We could kind of jump around doing things," recalls Pat Brymer, who was there for all of it, "and continuity was important. [Shari] had a thousand costumes for changes, but fortunately, the wardrobe lady (Molly Harris Campbell) was on top of it. She would prerecord a lot in the early morning or in the evening after she was done shooting. It was really hard work. She put in all the nightmare elements: she had children, animals, puppets. They all take time."

As with her other efforts, there was never any question who ran the show. "It was absolutely Shari's set," Williamson said. "It was her show; she dictated the hours, she dictated the schedule to a large degree with her stage manager, or what we call in film the A.D. [assistant director]. It was run the way she wanted it run."

"I think Mom preferred TV because she could control the edit," Mallory says, "whereas life does not have an edit button."

Stormy and Pat came before me in terms of having Mom's trust. She believed, and I believe, if you're going to have someone as your teacher and your mentor, listen to them. Trust them. Don't argue with them. Stormy respected Mom's musical talent and discipline as a student, and Mom had tremendous respect for Stormy. Also, Mom and Stormy traveled together for decades. After shows, they would have dinner; when there were marital issues, Mom would cry to Stormy. Stormy was the person she was on the road with.

—*Mallory*

"The thing I liked about Shari the most was that she was very admiring of other people's talent," Brymer says, "if it didn't cross hers, of course. I would rig the puppets for her and, on the Lamb Chops, I was able to do a monofilament string rig inside of her that didn't show at all, and I could make the arms articulate and go up to her face and chest—like a marionette, but from underneath. Shari would be on the tabletop and I would be down below her. There were a million strings coming out the bottom of Lamb Chop to do the different articulations. [Shari] was my biggest ally when we were filming because we had a couple of hard-assed directors who were not used to holding up production to do puppeteering, and they would occasionally get on the God mike[4] and say, 'Are we ready now?' Shari would sit there very patiently and say, 'Excuse me, when Pat is done, we'll let you know.'"

She memorized everything. Remember, she had to learn four parts: Lamb Chop, Charlie Horse, Hush Puppy, and her own lines. We never waited for her. It was very frustrating when we had guests stars who would show up and not know their lines. "What are you doing at night?" Mom would work all day, go home, take a bath, and study her lines; then go to bed, get up, and come back to the studio. It wasn't a job for her; it was a joy.

—*Mallory*

In January 1992 the first of eighty-six half-hour episodes went into production. The show was produced by Paragon Entertainment Corporation and presented by Chicago PBS affiliate WTTW. The creative team featured writers Lan O'Kun, Bernard Rothman, and Mallory Tarcher (later Lewis); music by Bob Golden and John Rodby; and direction by Michael Watt, Stan Wolf, and Michael Jacobson. Shari, Bernard Rothman, Jon Slan (head of Paragon), and Shawn Williamson were producers, and Pat Brymer was head puppeteer ("Because I only have two hands," Shari explained).

4. This refers to the public-address system wielded by the director, also known as VOG (Voice of God).

Lamb Chop's Play-Along grew out of the 1988 home video *Lamb Chop's Sing-Along Play-Along.* "Not the vignettes and not the music," Mallory says, "but all of the games, jokes, silly stunts, knock-knocks—those all arrived from my grandfather on little tiny pieces of paper and matchbook covers where he would write down a thought and stick it in the mail to Shari. That was my grandfather's show."

Perhaps the series' most memorable element, as well as its most irritating, at least for grown-ups, was the closing song. The opening theme was the spritely "It's Lamb Chop's Play-Along," but the earworm that burrowed into everyone's skull was the song that ran under the closing credits: "The Song that Doesn't End."

"Where does 'The Song that Doesn't End' come from?" rhetorically asks Norman Martin, who has the distinction of having written it. "I would have to say it comes from Nichols Canyon. And why? Because I was driving home one night and I took a turn off onto Nichols Canyon from Hollywood Boulevard. To the top of Nichols Canyon is 1.7 miles. I live in that area. Takes you about ten minutes to navigate. And as I turned onto Nichols Canyon, I heard 'This is the song that doesn't end.' Where it came from, I don't know. I know that by the time I got up to the top of the hill, there it was. I rushed into the house and I said, 'Everybody hush. I think I got a good song.' I wrote it down and there it was."

"It's funny," Mallory notes, "because people remember 'The Song that *Doesn't* End' as 'The Song that *Never* Ends.' . . . But since everybody sings it as 'never ends,' clearly that was a wrong lyric." Even the press gets it wrong. In her August 15, 1998, appreciation, the *Washington Post*'s Sharon Waxman waxes, "Give me spicy, silly, sparkling Shari Lewis any day, singing that signature tune that makes no particular sense but that neither my kids nor I can get out of our heads," and then proceeded to quote the wrong lyrics.[5]

Nevertheless (or should it be doesn't the less?), "The Song that Doesn't End" exemplifies the playfulness of the entire series. Each episode is full of games, puns, songs, magic tricks, factoids, and other

5. Wikipedia acknowledges both versions, calling the actual lyrics the "original version" and the misquoted lyrics the "classical variation." https://en.wikipedia.org/wiki/The_Song_That_Never_Ends.

take-aways. The shows were produced in segments not only to meet the attention spans of young viewers but also, as it turned out, to be able to mix and match them into theme-driven videos for later release by A&M Home Video.

"Shari sits down and she selects themes and then she'll specially select the segments to go along with those themes," remarked Regina Kelland, her A&M representative. "So the videos that are out in the marketplace are not just episodes taken off the television show." They are—and they have been issued on DVD as—freestanding programs. "And it's not just the safe stuff. I mean, she gets into personal relationships and sibling rivalry and hurt feelings and all of those other things that a child's world revolves around." But mostly, there is music. "Everybody's always said that music is the universal language," Stormy Sacks reports, "and Shari tries to perform through music and she uses music to teach and she uses music to expand a child's realm."

The show touched viewers in ways that ran the gamut. Mallory—recalling how her mother affected generations of kids—reports the full range: "We got some fan mail that just breaks your heart. Some of it was from people in prison (which was kind of scary, such as one man who said, 'I know you're my sister and you have the money.' He was in cell block six). Most, however, were just touching. But, of the emotionally touching letters, one was from a woman who wrote in and said that her son was autistic and he was five years old. And he had never spoken a word. And she came in from having made him breakfast and he was watching our show and he turned around and looked at her and pointed at the TV and said, 'Mommy! Lamb Chop!'"

Never content to recycle, Shari was demanding of her staff to create new stuff. Mallory was one of her writers and, eventually, her producer. "She let me take over," Mallory says. "I'm very organized. I have a producer's mind. Shawn Williamson ran the below-the-line, I ran the creative. Bernie Rothman would say, when we did *Play-Along,* 'We're running behind; your mother's taking too long.' I made a deal with Mom. I said, 'Look, every episode that we are on schedule for, I'm gonna give you $10,000 toward the next episode for you to do whatever the hell you want. If you're not on schedule, I need to keep that money so that I can pay for being late. But if we are on schedule I've got a slush fund that you can use for whatever you want.' These were the days when ChromaKey[6] cost $10,000 to throw something across a green screen. If she wanted a special effect or a pink elephant, I just had to have extra money. She was the best star ever, and all I wanted to do was be the best producer ever. We trusted each other. I trusted her to do the best performance, and she trusted me to run the show so that she *could* do the best performance. A producer is supposed to protect their star."

The episodes were shot on a variety of tape formats over the years before the advent of digital recording. They were edited offline by John Christie, Allan Pinvidic, and Don Thompson of Finale Editworks on the VHS system then in use, then onlined using master tapes so the final show met broadcast standards.

On only a few occasions did mother and daughter differ, and one of those occasions was when Shari attempted to do hip-hop, resurrecting Wing Ding, her long-retired hipster crow puppet. "Wing Ding was the beatnik," Mallory said. "One thing Mom wasn't was cool. She could do a lot of things, all good, but she was the least culturally cool person I have ever met. She couldn't pull off Wing Ding 'cause she just had no beat in her. The one piece I never used—we shot it for *Lamb Chop's Play-Along*—Mom was determined to do a hip-hop rap number. We shot it and I remember calling her from the edit bay and saying we're not using it. She said, 'I did it perfectly.' I said, 'Mom, you look like an idiot in red overalls. A sixty-one-year-old little Jewish lady? It's just wrong, Mom, it doesn't look good, you don't do it well.'"

"I was perfect, I hit every dance move."

"Mom, that's not the point. I'm not putting it in the show."

"You have to or we won't have enough time for the season."

"I'll use something twice."

"You can't do that."

6. Also called "green screen" (formerly "blue screen"), this is a method of superimposing people in a studio over a background shot elsewhere. Today it is the mainstay of special effects and can even be done on home computers, but when it was introduced, it was costly.

"Then you come up here and do it."

Once Shari saw her hip-hop performance, she agreed with Mallory. It never aired.

This is not to say that Shari took herself seriously, only her work. Pat Proft, writer of the *Police Academy* and *Hot Shots* comedies, recalls the time he cast Lamb Chop as an extra in *Wrongfully Accused,* his 1998 parody of *The Fugitive.* He was finishing the film in Vancouver, where *Play-Along* was being shot.

"I was in an elevator with Mallory," he says, "and I said, 'Can I use Lamb Chop for something?' Mallory may have been the one who manipulated Lamb Chop during the shoot that we ultimately did, but I got to meet Shari through a day of looping."

Adds Mallory, "It was kind of a shock to me when I offered Mom the opportunity of Lamb Chop being in a movie but because of scheduling she couldn't be there to do her. It was the first time she trusted me or anyone to do Lamb Chop without her present. In some ways, it was the beginning of the passing of the torch."

Continues Proft, "I was surprised she came in because [Mallory] coulda done it. But no, Shari Lewis came in to do the voice. She didn't want anyone else to do it. In fact, I think she put [the puppet] on when she did the looping. She wouldn't just do the voice. I remember talking with Shari and then checking with Lamb Chop: 'Are you ready?' This was a real person. Lamb Chop was a normal thing, a normal creature that can converse with you." Proft says, "It was very sweet to talk to [Shari] because she was just a very sweet lady. I remembered her from when I was a kid, from her show. It was like talking to a showbiz person, not a puppet person. Talking to Mister Rogers is one thing, but talking to Shari Lewis—this was someone who sang and danced and did stuff. She had a great love of kids and it was a fun couple-three hours."

The illusion of Lamb Chop's reality can be explained by the connection between ventriloquy and magic—the magician and ventriloquist communities are very close—as Jay Johnson explains. Jay and his puppet Bob were breakout stars on the ABC sitcom *Soap* in the 1970s. "I always compare magic and ventriloquism," he says. "Magic operates on an idea that you don't really know how that effect is being done, and even if you do know, you still appreciate it. In ventriloquism, you know what's gonna

> Mom liked things to move very fast, and she liked the cuts to be very fast, so as soon as she was done with a scene, she would make a face so the editor would have to cut. One time she had a little kitten in her hand when we did the same take ten times. At the end of the song the kitten meowed. I asked her, "How did you get the kitten to meow every time?" She said, "Oh, I just squeezed it with my fingernails." She was very practical.
>
> —*Mallory*

happen, you know who's doing it, they're doing it right in front of you, and psychologically you still want to go there." Johnson recalls an appearance he made on *The Mike Douglas Show,* where he told the straitlaced Douglas, "Now, Mike, don't treat Bob like an instrument and ask him questions like 'how do you work his head?' because he's gonna react like a human. Just treat him like another guest and that will work. Well, it does and it doesn't because the moment they treat him like another guest, this wooden head talks back and they're in an unfamiliar territory and they all wanna go, 'Oh, I'd better be a straight man and feed him lines.' It's part of this psychosis we put people through."

While Shari was taping her show, she continued to publish children's books, an activity she had begun in 1958 with *The Shari Lewis Puppet Book* (Citadel Press) and continued with Golden Books. Her first title was 1959's *Party in Shariland Featuring Shari and Her Puppets,* a Golden Book written not by her but by popular children's author Ann McGovern (*Stone Soup*). The book–TV show synergy didn't exist in the late 1950s; that didn't happen until the 1970s with the emergence of media conglomerates.

In 1961, possibly inspired by her 1958 marriage to nascent publisher Jeremy Tarcher, she began writing—or, in some cases, cowriting—a succession of books aimed at children that embraced the reading experience itself. This was as much a tribute to her father's "edutainment" ethic as it was an effort to establish her brand commercially. On that note, she wrote *Stories to Read Aloud* (Wonder Books), an anomaly in that it featured Wing Ding on the cover rather than Lamb Chop. Although she allowed Crosby Newell to write *The Shari Lewis Wonder Book* (Wonder

Books, 1961) without her, by 1962 she was back in control with *Folding Paper Puppets* (Stein & Day), coauthored with Lillian Oppenheimer. Over the next thirty-six years (until her death in 1998), she authored or coauthored upward of four dozen books, most of them with her solo byline but others shared with Jeremy, Lan O'Kun, Norman Martin, Marty Gold, and Lisa Goldrick. (Some of her collaborators may have forgone credit.) Her titles published by Holt, Rinehart & Winston ranged from fanciful (*Toy Store in a Book,* 1979) and functional (*Things Kids Collect,* 1980) to narrative (*Spooky Stuff,* 1979) and inspirational (*The Do It Better Book,* 1980). One of her most popular efforts was the One Minute series designed to address her young fans' short attention spans and encourage them to read out loud. The titles are self-explanatory: *One-Minute Bedtime Stories, One-Minute Animal Stories, One-Minute Easter Stories, One-Minute Fairy Tales, One-Minute Bible Stories (Old Testament),* and *One-Minute Bible Stories (New Testament).*

Typical of her process was Shari's collaboration with stage and screen star Florence Henderson. "Working with Shari Lewis was a unique experience," Henderson told Michael Rosen in an interview for the Television Academy shortly after Shari's death. "She was extremely bright and talented in so many areas and she called me. She said that she had done the project, *Children's Bible Stories,* a video and a book—she had done the Old Testament—and she wanted me to do the New Testament. So I would go to her house and we would work on the book and the series and we would do these one-minute Bible stories and I worked with Lamb Chop. It was a wonderful experience. She stood apart. She was so unique because she was so intelligent and so inventive. I think it's a great loss that Shari isn't with us because she created so many wonderful shows for children that adults could also enjoy—but did it before, really, anyone else was doing it."[7]

Shari turned out several children's books a year, each of which had to be illustrated, proofread, and prepared for publication. This was in addition to her duties on *Lamb Chop's Play-Along,* which first aired September 10, 1992. The broadcast competition was both stiff and strange. This was

7. Florence Henderson, interviewed by Michael Rosen, October 20 and 29, 1999, TelevisionAcademy.com.

the era of "Barney," PBS's purple dinosaur that drove everybody crazy except the preschool audience he was designed to captivate. Paragon president Jon Slan had more or less stumbled into the children's television market with Shari even before such programming was mandated by the Children's Television Act. When *Lamb Chop's Play-Along* took off, Slan and Shari—who had signed with powerhouse agency International Creative Management on the strength of her new series—began planning two other projects: *Cop and Chop,* an animated series for Lamb Chop created by Shari and composer Norman Martin, and *First Class,* a live-action concept by Shari and musician Stormy Sacks featuring real teachers and puppet students.[8] Neither project happened.

Meanwhile, Ann Hurwitz had been living in Florida with the assistance of a helper who visited on a regular basis. When the Tarchers deemed it time for Shari's mother to come live with them, they dispatched majordomo Georgia Anderson to Florida to bring Ann west and help her make the transition. Though only in her seventies, Ann was in decline, and she needed a wheelchair at airports. When Todd Tillson went to collect Ann and Georgia, he was in for a surprise. "I went to pick them up at LAX," he recalls, "and here they come toward me, and they're both in wheelchairs. Georgia had developed some condition, perhaps fibromyalgia, and she couldn't walk. It was just such a sight."

Once Ann became ensconced with the Tarchers, Todd's duties were expanded to include driving her to various doctor appointments. Ann had already survived half a dozen operations for brain tumors, but it was a recurring problem and she was becoming weaker and weaker. In addition, she may have begun descending into dementia and could no longer censor her speech. "It was somewhat mortifying to Shari," Todd says, referring to Ann's use of racially insensitive language. "It wasn't that [Ann and Shari] didn't have discord about certain sociopolitical stuff," but that didn't include "being vulgar and . . . spewing it out." Ann died on April 8, 1984.

Eight months after her mother's death and thirteen years after her father's death, Shari achieved something of which her parents would have been proud: she opened on Broadway. *Lamb Chop on Broadway* debuted

8. "Shari Lewis Talks Chop with Paragon," *Variety,* August 23, 1993.

on December 8 at the Richard Rodgers Theatre for a limited run, just in time for the Christmas tourist season. Directed by Kevin Carlisle, the show included music by Stormy Sacks, lyrics by Rob Battan, and a book by Saul Turteltaub (spelled "Sol" in the program), with additional music by Norman Martin, Lan O'Kun, and Cliff Jones. The family-oriented sketch show featured not only Shari and her hand puppets but also "Big Lamb Chop," "Big Charlie Horse," and "Big Hush Puppy" played and danced by KathyJo Boss, Guy Woodson, and Jeff Drew, respectively. The set was a barnyard, with the musicians upstage behind a picket fence. Far from being lost in the 1,400-seat theater, Shari held her own.

"It's basically a one-woman show," said Turteltaub. "She has Lamb Chop, Charlie Horse, and Hush Puppy in the show, but she is all those voices and she has to memorize all those parts. So it's staggering how much she can memorize, [but] I guess [it] goes back to the academics of her mother." Norman Martin added at the time, "She'll be using a lot of new material, a lot of old material. I've been writing some stuff for her."

"This is a one-woman show with a cast of thousands," Shari explained while Lamb Chop listened, just waiting to speak. "There are three dancers."

"One is a Lamb Chop," interrupts Lamb Chop.

"One is a Lamb Chop," Shari agrees. "And one is—"

"Hush Puppy."

"Yes, and one is—"

"Charlie Horse!"

"Yes," Shari says.

To which Lamb Chop adds, "That's it."

"And it's wonderful dancing with Lamb Chop," Shari says, looking at her puppet hand. "I love it."

"You missed it all these years," Shari's hand says back to her.

"Yes," she says wistfully, "I did miss it all these years."

It was up to Brymer to work out the mechanics of the human-sized characters. Mindful of the discomfort endured by the big-headed furry cast members at Disney theme parks, Brymer designed the costumes for Big Lamb Chop, Big Hush Puppy, and Big Charlie Horse with their inhabiters' comfort in mind. "There was a viewing screen inside the mouth on Lamb Chop that you couldn't see," he said, "because it was set back so far, but they could see through it and they could breathe air through it, and then there was a vent on the top of the head underneath all the curls, and then the eyelashes were made out of a very porous foam so they could also breathe through that and the performer could see through the eyelashes. I used to have to wear those characters and I knew how miserable they could be, so I tried to make them as comfortable as possible. We had body pods in them that would come out, and they had nylon hoops inside, and we could take the hoops out and the whole thing could be thrown in the washer and cleaned. That's where all the perspiration went." All three human-size suits had the same amenities.

Lamb Chop's Play-Along had wrapped production and was airing to success on PBS stations across America and would continue to do so until 1997. Shari, however, was looking for her next television venue. It would be her last.

14

Pizza to Go

The Charlie Horse Music Pizza was a follow-up to *Lamb Chop's Play-Along.* Shari got the idea for this diverse, multicultural show during a conversation with Jeremy during which it hit them that children like music, pizza, and the beach, so why not combine all three? It became a family affair. Shari and Jeremy got "created by" credit and Bernard Rothman, Mallory, and Shari "developed" the show, meaning that they made the Tarchers' creation work.

Mallory, however, had doubts going in. "I never thought *Music Pizza* was a good idea. PBS was trying to expand its age range to eight- to twelve-year-olds. The shows were written on a music level that was aiming at that. But eight- to twelve-year-olds don't watch puppets and don't watch PBS. I always thought it was amusing, I just never thought it was a great show concept."

"The greatest surprise for me," Shari told blogger Kira Albin in 1997, "is working with my daughter, who is creative supervisor, head writer, and producer of certain aspects of everything I do. It's just wonderful working with your family."[1]

With food in mind, the first person they brought aboard was Dom DeLuise, who was not only an old friend from Music & Art High School but also a nonpareil comic actor and celebrated Italian cook. "He was a generous, kind man," Mallory says. "Dom would tell the young actor he was playing the scene with to 'roll your eyes this way' or 'look this way' and you'll get the biggest laugh. He would give other people the laugh."

1. Kira Albin, "Shari Lewis in the Lamb Light," *Grandtimes,* 1997, www.grandtimes.com /lambchop.html.

"Dom DeLuise was awesome," agrees Shawn Williamson, who was one of the show's producers. "Bernie Rothman and Shari would select casts. We had Pat Morita—I can't remember if it was a Passover special or Hanukkah—Pat Morita, for me, was like working with a superstar because of *The Karate Kid*. Alan Thicke was in a number of shows, and he was great; he was friends with Bernie. Jan Rubes, who was an amazing actor, who had been in *Witness*, played sort of a creepy guy in a Halloween special. But Dom DeLuise was the most spectacular."

In addition to DeLuise playing pizza maker "Cookie," the mixed (puppet and human) cast included Chancz Perry as "Takeout," who delivered pizzas by skateboard; an orangutan in a suit created by Pat Brymer; Wezley Morris[2] as "Junior," the show's male ingenue; Doug Cameron, one of Canada's most popular actors, as the music store owner; Gordon Robertson as the voice of "Fingers," a purple raccoon from Brymer's workshop; Dan Joffe; and Chantal Strand.

Shari's philosophy behind *The Charlie Horse Music Pizza* was a continuation of her father's teachings. "Listening to music is one thing," she said, "but *participating* in the making of music is introducing you to the integrated power that only comes from music lessons. Group lessons are fine, but I do as much as I can by making everything participatory. So it's not like studying an instrument. It's not like facing something that you don't know how to do at all and then realizing that if you stick to it, you'll get it. And that calm applies to everything. It helps you with relationships. Musically it's very sophisticated, but lyrically I'm very conscious of reducing language so that the terminology is very clear. That's the game I play."

Colman DeKay, a young veteran with an impressive resumé, was hired to write the series. "The first thing I told her," DeKay said, "was, 'You know, you're responsible for my first erection.' And she said, 'If I had a dime for everybody that's told me that, I wouldn't have to do this show.' I loved her."

DeKay was Mallory's discovery; the two of them had met at the wedding of mutual friends (where Shari killed with a toast). "Then," he says, "a couple weeks later I get a call from Mallory saying, 'Hi, it's Mallory

2. Not to be confused with Wesley Morris, the Pulitzer Prize–winning film critic.

Lewis, do you remember me from the wedding?' and I said, 'Yes,' and she said, 'Well, I remember you because you were very funny and you didn't spill. Would you like to work for my mother?' and I said, 'Of course.'"

The final word, naturally, came from Shari. Asked to write an audition script, DeKay decided to test Shari as much as he expected her to test him. He recalls, "I went away and deliberately did this four-page run where all the characters were in it and all the characters were finishing each other's sentences—line, line, line, line, line, back, back, back, back—to mess with her, to see if she could do it, right? I finished the script. I didn't email it to her, I printed it and went over to her house for the table reading; there was this little table, and I handed her the script cold. She hadn't seen it. She starts reading—of course, she's reading everything, all the characters—and she's doing the facial stuff with her hand with no puppet on it. These very specific moves. I'm waiting for her to get to the tricky scene, the joke scene. She gets to it and she sees that it's going to be this long run, and she just HITS it, cold, and does it perfect the first time. I'm going, 'My God, this is something I've never seen.' She gets through it and then she looks at me like, 'You son of a bitch.' We hit it off from that moment."

Some writers consider it a comedown to do a children's show after a career penning for adults. Not DeKay. "Comedy is comedy. One thing

---

I would lose myself in that sock. Completely credible. I would look at it, except when I was looking to see if Shari's mouth was moving, and it never was. What was really illuminating was seeing her hands work without a sock puppet. Her fingers would work in a certain way, and you could tell if the character was sad or angry or teasing the other character. She could articulate that without the character on her hand. And-and-and when I tried to trick her that first time, she not only spot-on had the rhythm, but her hands were moving and expressing. And most of the time she had both hands moving because she would have two characters, and her voice would change. I think there were four or five characters in that one scene. She would inhabit each character on the split second.

—Colman DeKay

Shari never did was pander to children. She never spoke down to them ever, ever, ever, ever. That was one of her great qualities and so, for me, it was fun. She was a really very smart, very aware adult doing shows for children as an adult."

On *Music Pizza,* Charlie Horse was the star. Surprisingly, Lamb Chop didn't seem to mind. "At six she doesn't think very much," Shari told a reporter. "Charlie Horse said something funny the other day. Somebody asked him how did it happen that after all these years he got his name above the title on one of my shows. And he said, 'I changed agents.'"

Having proved herself and gained her mother's trust on *Lamb Chop's Play-Along,* Mallory was handed more authority on *The Charlie Horse Music Pizza.* "We had a system," she says, "where, first draft, she could make any notes she wanted. John Christie and our other editors and I all worked together so long and nobody didn't want to make her happy, nobody wanted a bad product, she knew that."

Again, Shari collected her production team, and again she expected public broadcasters to step up. This time, they did not. When the per-episode cost of the series hit $250,000 (versus $90,000 to $110,000 for *Play-Along*), PBS balked. "It was the most expensive show Mom ever had," Mallory says. "She always told people, 'One day I'm gonna get a show that has a real budget and I'm gonna pay you well,' and she did."

The Public Broadcasting Service is a gauntlet for producers; some have called it a tar pit. That's its dirty secret. While everyone extols the programming, many who have tried to work with PBS (except perhaps Ken Burns) quickly learn that they must raise money from a variety of sources to bankroll their show, and then they are at the mercy of individual stations to air it. There is no automatic pickup, as with a broadcast or cable network; that's why it's called the Public Broadcasting *Service,* not the Public Broadcasting *System.* PBS stations acknowledge the "generous support of our viewers," and donors think their contributions fund the making of their favorite programs, but in reality, that money is used to air the shows locally and pay the salaries of station employees.

Despite the struggle, Shari remained pragmatic. "We live in a commercial world," she said when plans were first announced for *Music Pizza.* "Everything that I have ever done has been a part of that commercial world, including PBS. PBS gives me a very small fraction of the money and I have to raise the rest. But there are people now who are beginning to be aware of their responsibilities: social ventures networks, people who are conscious. They come in all shapes. This is no New Age venture. People are beginning to be more conscious of that. What has made the difference is that when people put on educational TV shows they generally do it because they are pressured to do it and their intention is not good. Their desires are good, but not their [motives], and that's why the shows come out boring. Then it's no wonder that they don't succeed. At PBS, people who are doing the shows have the most wholesome intentions I have ever seen. They never tell me what to do in order to reach the lowest common denominator."

Mallory's private take, in retrospect, was different: "I thought it was like trying to sell dolls to twelve-year-olds. People have often asked me, 'Are kids different today than fifty years ago?' No. I don't think children from zero to five are any different, but I *do* think children from six up are *very* different. My son was building Minecraft at six. Are toddlers different? No. They need the same learning skills. But with maturity, interest has accelerated, so I just never particularly thought the concept was sound and I never thought the target market was sound. I think the show was great, I just think it should have been a show for four- to six-year-olds."

> She would be at the studio first thing in the morning. She and I used to do battle over who could get there first. Finally, Shawn Williamson took us aside and said, "You may *not* come until seven. You're making the craft service lady cry."
>
> —*Mallory*

Nevertheless, eager to start production by the fall of 1997 for a planned January 5, 1998, premiere date, Shari focused all her energies on finding new financing. Putting into practice her wont to teach music, she approached the National Association of Music Merchants (NAMM) and Remo, the drumhead manufacturer, for underwriting. NAMM is a trade association for the music industry that "strengthens the $17 billion global music, sound and event technology products industry," according to its mission statement, and its "trade shows serve as the crossroads for professionals wanting to seek out the newest innovations in music, recording technology, sound, stage and lighting products." Remo, founded in 1957 by Remo D. Belli, innovated Mylar drumheads and is a leading manufacturer of that percussive instrument.

It wasn't enough. When the underwriters' combined involvement hit a financial shortfall, Shari did the unthinkable: she sold her company, Shari Lewis Enterprises. It was not pleasant. Things began to unravel.

For years, Shari had enjoyed a close relationship with Golden Books, the publisher of children's literature previously known as Western Publishing. Her manager Jim Golden (no relation to Golden Books), of the management company Management III, handled the affairs of Shari Lewis Enterprises. When PBS cut its commitment prior to production and Shari needed money to finance *The Charlie Horse Music Pizza,* she made the tough decision to sell Shari Lewis Enterprises to Golden Books.

As the acquisition was being worked out, licensing specialist Gary Hymowitz, who worked for Golden Books, was given an office in the Tarcher-Lewis home. He is still a close family friend. He observed that "Jim [Golden] was basically Shari's right hand in business aspects." As such, he had warned Shari in 1985 that her 1957 and 1960 copyrights for Lamb Chop were about to expire and needed to be renewed, but Jeremy assured her that all was well as, prior to Golden, he had been handling those issues.[3] When Golden Books conducted its normal due diligence prior to the sale, however, it discovered that the copyrights had indeed lapsed, and Lamb Chop had fallen into the Public Domain. Consequently, Golden Books sharply reduced the buyout price.

3. Prior to the controversial Copyright Extension Act of 1998, a US copyright lasted for twenty-eight years and could be renewed by the copyright holder or by his or her estate for another twenty-eight years. Accordingly, Shari's 1957 and 1960 copyrights would have needed to be renewed in 1985 and 1988, respectively. The 1983 registration of "new material" complicated the situation but did not reverse it. The 1998 law (sometimes called the Sonny Bono Copyright Act in honor of the late musician and congressman) provides copyright protection for the life of the author plus seventy years or for the life of a corporate author (usually a "work for hire") for ninety-five years from registration. The controversy comes from the work-for-hire provision, which runs counter to artists' rights everywhere else in the world.

The sale of Shari Lewis Enterprises to Golden Books was not the end of the corporate road for Lamb Chop and her family. A man named Eric Ellenbogen had a great deal to do with it, even though they never met. A Harvard and UCLA graduate who combined keen business acumen with a passion for nostalgia, he was a player in the merger madness of the 1990s that concentrated the power of the media into fewer and fewer hands. In 1987 Ellenbogen headed Broadway Video, which held the assets of Lorne Michaels, the producer of *Saturday Night Live*. In November 1998 Ellenbogen moved to Marvel Enterprises and stayed there until July 1999. At the same time, Golden Books was in financial trouble, and this drew Ellenbogen's attention.

"After Golden fell into bankruptcy the second time," says Gary Hymowitz, who was at Golden Books at the time, "Eric had gone to a different firm and reacquired the entertainment assets of Golden through the bankruptcy court. Random House acquired all the publishing assets. It was a joint deal that Eric had masterminded between Random House and himself, in that he would acquire all the rights to the entertainment assets and Random House acquired all the publishing assets. There was some crossover, with some long-term agreement that Random would maintain all the publishing in the acquisition, even in the entertainment brands, and Classic Media—the name of the new venture—had acquired all the entertainment rights and had a first look at the Random House rights. It was typical Eric: brilliant."

"I remember that being a really ugly and contentious part of the negotiation," says Hymowitz, who was supervising the plush toy aspects of the deal and wasn't involved in the back-and-forth. "The closing date kept moving because of it. It angered Shari and her husband and Mallory at the time. It was not unusual for things like that to happen to a lot of people who didn't have a full-time person checking copyright registrations."

According to staff members at Shari Lewis Enterprises, as soon as the sale closed, Golden Books' lawyers swooped in and made them sign agreements binding them to the publisher and preventing them from removing any property from the house or setting up deals elsewhere.

Ellenbogen also went after the Rankin & Bass animated TV specials (e.g., *Rudolph the Red-Nosed Reindeer*) and the UPA cartoon library (e.g., *Mr. Magoo, Gerald McBoing-Boing*). "That was all of his childhood memories that he was reacquiring. He set up Classic Media, and I went with that acquisition, and all of Golden Books Family Entertainment wound up at Classic Media. He flipped [Classic Media] numerous times in that period to investment corporations when he wanted more funding for additional acquisitions. He acquired entertainment rights at that point—a company out of the UK—and Veggietales, a Christian company out of Memphis. And then he flipped the entire company to DreamWorks, and then DreamWorks got acquired by NBC/Universal. I'm sure when DreamWorks acquired it they probably didn't even know that Lamb Chop was part of it. And the same way when NBC acquired DreamWorks, Lamb Chop got buried in all of that."

—*Gary Hymowitz*

Thus did the financing for *The Charlie Horse Music Pizza* come together, practically at gunpoint, and at the cost of Shari giving up everything she had built. In essence, she was back to square one.

Even when things looked bleak, Shari stayed loyal to her friends. When she asked Sonny Gordon to write an episode, she held her ground. "What I didn't know was that the producer [Bernie Rothman] did not want me to write the episode," Gordon says. "Not personal, but he had somebody else in mind to write this particular episode. She stood firm and said, 'He's gonna do it or I'm not gonna do the show.' When I turned in the first draft, Shari didn't make too many changes. I think Bernie might have made a few but, again, she always had my back. Always."

The Charlie Horse Music Pizza started preproduction in a Los Angeles TV studio before moving to Vancouver, as had *Lamb Chop's Play-Along*. The first season was going well, as expected. During a writing hiatus midway through the season, Mallory became pregnant. Consistent with the unofficial rules of women who worked in television, the conception was timed so that Mallory and her husband Brad Hood's son, Jamie, would be born during a hiatus.

After the break, production resumed with all the scripts prepared, all the songs prerecorded, all the sets dusted off, and the full Vancouver crew back to work. The first two episodes after the break went according to schedule, but when it was time to do the third, something was wrong: For the first time in her life, Shari wasn't ready.

15

The Silence of the Lamb

Shari wasn't herself. Pat Brymer was the first to notice. "She looked sick and she complained to me a number of times because I was always right underneath her or behind her," he says. "She would say that she hadn't been able to eat and hadn't been able to have bowel movements and she'd had one little thing after another. I thought, this is not boding well. We didn't even finish the third show. She had to go back to Los Angeles, so they gave everybody a two-week hiatus."

Judy Wexler also noticed that her boss was losing weight. "She wasn't fat but she was zaftig," she says. "Adorable, but zaftig; she was not a skinny girl. She was getting thinner and thinner. She loved the way she looked. I'm thin and I've gone through stages where I lose weight, and I just fly to the doctor." Shari made appointments with several gynecologists and, perhaps, chose the one whose diagnosis fit her wishes rather than the stark truth.

"Mom was not eating and she was not well," reports Mallory, who was producing the show. "Did she know she was ill? Probably, because she did not feel good. Did she think it was anything life-threatening? No, she was indomitable. The day before we were to begin shooting, I said, 'You need to go to the doctor; there's something wrong.'" When she hesitated, Mallory told her mother, "'I'm going to shut down the show until you go to the doctor.' She said, 'No, you can't shut down the show,' and I said, 'I'm the producer, yes I can.' So she went to the doctor, called me at eleven o'clock in the morning, and said, 'I just found out I have terminal cancer and six weeks to live. I will be at the studio at 1:00 p.m. this afternoon. No red eyes.'"

The diagnosis was uterine cancer. And as she had done with her breast cancer, Shari took control of her health and insisted on doing the thing she had done all her life: work. Whether that made her a pragmatist, fantasist, heroine, or whatever, it was her way of dealing with her fate, and it affected everyone around her, even though, for forty-eight hours, she withheld the news from most of them.

"The last day that we shot, oddly enough," recounts Brymer, "the final song she did was 'Hello-Goodbye.' It was written for the show, but not for that reason. I was the only one besides Todd Tillson who knew that she had this horrible cancer. It was Mallory that told us when she was diagnosed and said, 'My mother doesn't want anyone else to know.' Shari didn't even know that I knew. At the end I was practically in tears under the table because we knew that this was going to be it."

Almost certainly Shari knew that this would be her final appearance on camera. Soon, so did those closest to her. "June 17, 1998, was her last moment onstage," says Mallory, "and I remember buzzing down from the booth and saying, 'Mom, we don't need this song,' because I quite frankly didn't think I could stand to see my mother, who I knew was dying, sing 'good-bye' in the camera to me. But she looked into the camera and said, 'Oh, no, darling, you're gonna need this song.' And moms are always right, right? On the last day of shooting, she could not separate Charlie Horse's voice from Lamb Chop's voice. We did like six takes, and she couldn't keep them separate. I went up to her, I looked her in the eyes, and I said, 'That's it, Mom, we got it.' She looked at me and said, 'Is it gonna come out okay in the edit?' And I looked at her and I said, 'I promise.'"

"There were a couple of things that I witnessed at the end," Tillson describes. "She had developed a problem. It was very apparent because

---

The last words she spoke to me on the phone, after we had talked for twenty minutes, were, "Okay, I gotta go. I'm naked right now and I gotta go to a party." Don't need that image! Those were the last words I heard her say. I had seen her in November 1997 and she didn't look right. I figured something was wrong. She said she was gonna have surgery, but she didn't go into it. From what little she did say, I put two and two together. I didn't know how sick she was.

—*Heidi Hubbs*

> Brad gave Mom her last laugh. We were in the hospital and Mom was a day, maybe two before dying. A bunch of doctors came in. I was already in the room. One doctor said, "I'm Doctor so-and-so," another one said, "I'm Doctor so-and-so," and "I'm Doctor so-and-so." Brad followed them in and said, "I'm not a doctor but I play one on TV." It was literally Mom's last laugh.
>
> —*Mallory*

she was not vital in appearance. I think they were able to cover, but her stomach was this big, bulbous thing. When she got ready to come back to the hotel and we were getting ready to fly out, I went into her dressing room to pick up a few things and collect whatever I could and—this is really symbolic—I saw the last outfit she was wearing on camera, and there it was laying in a heap in the middle of the floor. It was never like her. She would never leave anything on the floor, and it was telling that she did the best she could to get out of it and get out of there."

Shari had beaten cancer once before. But not this time. Now she had to tell her crew. "People knew what was happening," Shawn Williamson said, "so there were many tears onstage. Many of the crew had been together for years prior to us shutting down—on and off with different specials and then *Lamb Chop's Play-Along* and the two years of *Charlie Horse.* She did make an announcement that was very emotional to the cast and crew. I remember that vividly and it was very emotional and very heartfelt. The next day she flew home."

Says Brymer, "When we finished, she went to her dressing room and the stage manager said, 'Now everybody get out on the main set. Shari wants to come back out and speak to you.' I said, 'Here it comes.' She came out on the set and sat down in a chair. She was a strong lady but she was almost in tears. All the crew was looking forward to the rest of the season. She came back out and told everybody that she hated to do it but her doctor had told her that she could not go on any longer and she had to go back to Los Angeles and they would have to cease production. It was heartbreaking. I was standing in one of the doorways and, as she left the stage, she walked by me and she said, 'Oh, Pat.' That was all she said. And that was the last I saw of her."

Todd Tillson continues. "She said, 'I'm gonna have to take a break for a while, I'm sorry.' They were going to finish up all the odds and ends. My wife Susan was there doing her job. Brad, Mallory's husband—and I certainly cut a lot of slack to him—suddenly became the alpha male in the sense of taking care of his in-laws. I came back with Shari and Jeremy, and then she went in for extreme cancer [treatment]."

Shari and Jeremy bought a house in Malibu [on the Pacific Coast Highway]. Brad and Mallory were living there at the time and looking after it. The idea was that it would be Shari and Jeremy's beach getaway, but then everything went the way it went. This one time I went out there with Mallory, and Shari and Jeremy came too. Shari was quite frail at the time, like a little fledgling bird. They all went out and sat on the deck with their chairs facing over the water. I was in the kitchen. I looked over and I thought, "Wow, there's a priceless shot." All I was thinking about was capturing it for Jeremy and Mallory. I got my camera and took a couple of shots from a side angle so you could see the essence of the three of them looking out at the water.

—Todd Tillson

"Like most mothers and daughters, we had had a difficult period while one of us was a teenager," says Mallory. "I was very lucky that I got to know and work with my mother as an adult and I got to appreciate her as both a talent and a human being, and she, as me, for the same. The last thing my mother said when she stepped off the stage—to a standing ovation, of course—was, 'You were the producer of my lifetime and I was so lucky to have you.' She was right, but I hold that compliment and acknowledgment close, as she would not have said it if she didn't mean it."

Six months prior, Shari had had a hysterectomy when an examination revealed fibroids. Says Mallory, still upset at the process, "It turned up questionable results. Mom insisted we tell no one until we had confirmation. One doctor said it was terminal cancer, then Sloan-Kettering and another couple of high-ritzy places said it was not, and then she got cleared by the studio doctor for insurance purposes, so the family assumed all was well and we proceeded with shooting. It turned out the original diagnosis was correct."

"It's a day I'll never forget," adds Richard Seymour, "probably the most emotional day except for [losing] my parents. After we were done shooting this number, [Shari] gathered everyone around her on the soundstage and—you know, Shari was a tough-as-nails kind of gal, right? So to see her get emotional in any way was kind of shocking and unusual. But in a very emotional speech she announced that they're shutting down production, that she has stage four cancer, terminal cancer, and she said—I'll paraphrase what she said—'You all know I'm not a religious person but I really need your prayers.' Nobody could hold back their tears. It was a very, very emotional day. She wasn't a sentimental type of person. When we came back from Vancouver and I was in the office

---

The day after Mom told the cast and crew she was dying and had to go home, she and my dad prepared to leave Vancouver. She had seven suitcases. Shawn Williamson arrived to take her to the airport, as did our six drivers/production assistants (PAs). They were all in suits standing outside of their cars or vans. Shawn took my parents, and each of the PAs took one suitcase. Brad and I came downstairs to see them off. It was one of the most moving and memorable experiences of my life.

—*Mallory*

We created our son on the night we were told Mom had terminal cancer. We had been pregnant, then four days later had a miscarriage. We had to wait a month, and then I was fertile again, so Brad flew up to Vancouver from Los Angeles while all this drama was going on with Mom being diagnosed and having six weeks to live. We go back to the hotel, and I'm like, "Okay, let's go," and he goes, "Really?" and I go, "Yeah. Fertile. We're trying to make a baby." Good performer that he is—the climax of that experience—Brad said, "You know, we just made a baby," and I said, "I know." And then I don't think we had sex for weeks.

—*Mallory*

and she was going to begin treatment, she said to me, 'Isn't it a bummer?' That was her way of dealing with life. Instead of getting all weepy and sad [she said], 'This is a bummer, isn't it?'"

Back in Los Angeles, when it came time to make what would be her last trip to the hospital, Todd drove Shari and Jeremy to Cedars-Sinai. "Shari was sitting behind me," he remembers. "We were in Jeremy's Mercedes. He had gotten out of the passenger side to go in and get the crew to come out and take Shari upstairs and all that, and there was this brief moment when we were sitting there together and I kinda turned a little sideways so she wouldn't feel totally cut off, and we're sitting there quietly and I can't think of anything to say, and I'm trying to be calm and just be there for her. All of a sudden, she says, 'Well, Todd, it's been really nice knowing you.' That just about gutted me right there. That meant the world to me, and I wanted to have some wonderful, quick response, but all I could say was, 'I love you, Shari.' Then the doors came crashing open and out came the crew, and they got her upstairs and I brought the luggage up."

Shari underwent chemotherapy. Her publicist, Maggie Begley, floated a story that she was responding well, but the cancer didn't know it and continued apace.

"She was in the hospital," Mallory recalls, "and I came to the hospital with the first ultrasound [of the baby]. I had a picture of Jamie. Mom had just come out of surgery. She came back to the room and she couldn't catch her breath, she couldn't breathe. I went slamming into the hallway saying, 'Somebody get back in here.' They told me to calm down and I told them that was not going to happen until somebody came in there. And as they came in and they put the oxygen over her face, she pushed them away. She looked at me and said, 'I want you to know how happy I am about the baby and how much I love you.' And then she closed her eyes and that was the last thing she said to me. It was everything you could want." Shari slipped into a coma.

Mallory drove home knowing that her mother would be given palliative care until she could return to the hospital to be with her. Unfortunately, pneumonia set in first. Shari Lewis died on Sunday, August 2, 1998, at 6:12 p.m. She died alone. Jeremy was not with her. Mallory, still upset, says, "He pulled the plug on Mom. On the phone. From the house.

He was right to pull the plug—she was gone—but he let her die alone. When I said, 'Why weren't you there?' he said, 'It could have taken hours.' They were together forty-odd years. He sat at home to watch a football game and let Mom die alone and didn't tell me. I said, 'Why didn't you tell me? I would have been with her.' He said, 'Well, you're pregnant, I didn't want to upset you.' Such a coward."

Shari was cremated and her ashes were given to Mallory. On Sunday, August 9, the family held a memorial at the Writers Guild Theatre in Beverly Hills. As the mourners entered the auditorium, everyone was given a tiny Lamb Chop finger doll as a memento. Mallory produced the video tributes.[1]

"I got invited to her memorial service," says Carla Rhodes. "I didn't know I was that close to her. I went to her house, too, which was very sad, because I thought when I went to her house it would be to visit her, not to mourn her."

But that's not the end of the story. Ironically, Shari's fate may have been decided ten years earlier when she took the cancer drug Tamoxifen. Although Tamoxifen can be useful for treating breast cancer, it was later discovered that the drug can promote the development of endometrial and other cancers, including cancer of the uterus.

For weeks after her death, the staff at her house fielded countless calls and messages from friends, fans, and colleagues. "I was overwhelmed by the outpouring of love that came in to the office that whole week," says Richard Seymour. "I can't even begin to tell you the people that called crying on the phone. I don't mean this in a facetious way, but I really became like a grief counselor for people, particularly Jeremy, after Shari died. He was crying every day. I was there to offer whatever comfort I could and listen to him."

Of course, Shari's passing was noted by the media. Typical of the newspaper tributes was the one by Richard Severo of the *New York Times,* who wrote on August 4, "Ms. Lewis was acknowledged to have all the instincts of a multifaceted entertainer. Although she was never a schoolteacher, she knew how to reach children with her puppet sidekicks,

1. The postproduction crew cobbled together three episodes of *Music Pizza* from the material completed before Shari's death.

chief among them being Lamb Chop, an ageless curly-haired creature who would interrupt Ms. Lewis with all manner of observations and questions. Lamb Chop was arguably her most beloved puppet, but in the eyes of children who watched her shows, Charlie Horse and Hush Puppy weren't far behind."

Wrote Myrna Oliver in the August 4 edition of the *Los Angeles Times*, "Although she was known as a children's entertainer, Lewis also delighted nightclub crowds in Southern California and in Las Vegas, often with Donald O'Connor. Her act typically included distinct segments such as puppets named Zsa Sivero and Phyllis comparing measurements and the unending search for men; Lewis dancing with a life-size replica of Fred Astaire; and curly-lashed Lamb Chop in adult mode, tipsy and searching for a martini. Lamb Chop always appeared, at one time aspiring to be a *Playboy* bunny, complete with long floppy ears attached."

And this from *Playbill*, the magazine for theatergoers: "Farewell to entertainer Shari Lewis, the puppeteer best known for her long-running Saturday morning TV show. The creator of Lamb Chop, Charlie Horse, and Hush Puppy died of cancer Aug. 2. She'd been diagnosed with the disease in June and had been rallying—and planning episodes for her latest television show—before her death. Lewis and company appeared at the Richard Rodgers Theatre, Dec. 6–11, 1994, in *Lamb Chop on Broadway*, a family-oriented comedy scripted by Sol [*sic*] Turteltaub with songs by Stormy Sacks and Rob Battan." On top of that, she was deemed the "First Lady of American Ventriloquism" by the *Encyclopedia of Puppetry Arts*.

Mom's time on Broadway was one of the happiest and saddest times of her life. The show went woefully over budget (not entirely her fault, as the union rules and costs were obscene), and ticket sales were poor. She was up against the likes of *The Lion King*, and the ticket price was the same. And unlike Mom, people couldn't watch *The Lion King* on PBS every morning. We had to "paper the house," and the show closed quickly. Getting a one-woman (plus body suits) show on Broadway was her dream, but it didn't turn out as she expected. True to Mom's style, she had one night of crying and moved on.

—*Mallory*

Over the next year, Shari's staff was tasked with closing the office and packing her archives. Housekeeper Georgia Anderson retired and returned to her familial home in Richmond, Virginia. Although she visited Los Angeles to help Mallory and Brad when their son, Jamie, was born, within two years she had succumbed to Alzheimer's disease.

Shari had been a one-person industry. Once she was gone and her assets had been sold to a conglomerate with no advocate to remind the public of her legacy, her recognition began to fade. Plush Lamb Chops could still be found in toy stores, but as licenses for *Lamb Chop's Play-Along* and *The Charlie Horse Music Pizza* ran out (and as digital TV rendered their analog technology less attractive for reruns), Shari Lewis risked becoming merely a memory.

Those who had worked for Shari knew that their services would no longer be needed, but what happened next was a surprise. "I came in one afternoon," says Todd Tillson. "It was just Jeremy and me. We walked back to the little round table by the sliding glass doors looking at the pool. It's very quiet and he sort of sat there, hat in hand, hoping that I would understand. He said, 'Look, I can't be alone. I know a lot of people are going to hate me for this, I haven't grieved enough for them and haven't given it enough time to satisfy them, but I need somebody in my life.' And that's when he told me." Jeremy was going to marry Judith Paige Mitchell, a true-crime writer and novelist who had become a successful television producer. "This was, at the most, a couple of weeks after Shari had passed," Tillson continues. "He was looking for me to have an understanding. I left without any judgment. I remember, towards the end [with Shari], at some point Shari said to me, 'Take care of Jeremy.' There was a sense that that comment was made for whatever reason. I heard him out and then excused myself and went home." Jeremy and Judith married in 1999.

The shadow of Shari, however, continued to haunt Tillson. In November 1999 he received a call from the staffers who had remained behind to empty the office. They asked him to help load Shari's papers and tapes from her storage facility in Hollywood into a Ryder truck. He was horrified when they drove the truck to a landfill in Eagle Rock. "I said, 'What the hell are you doing?' They said, 'We're just going on the directive of Jeremy. He wants us to empty out these things and take them to the dump.' I started pulling out as much as I possibly could, like her personal file, which I still have, and a number of things. I packed my Toyota like the Beverly Hillbillies and took it over to my storage unit and schlepped it around forever." Adds Tillson, "It was one of Shari's biggest personal concerns. She claimed not to be nostalgic or sentimental, but that was a big lie. The one time that she did open up to me . . . she said she feared that . . . all of her life and career [would] . . . end up relegated to a landfill. I thought, 'That will never happen.' But when I was there and started looking at these boxes, I said, 'You can't throw this away. What the hell are you thinking?'"

Richard Seymour has a different memory. "I was the one responsible ultimately for getting rid of practically everything; there were so many things over in storage. Todd may have gone to a landfill but I knew there were some things we just had to get rid of but I didn't personally throw it away. Whatever was saved was Mallory's."

Mallory was thankful when magician David Copperfield, an old family friend, offered to store the master tapes, awards, and program material in his Las Vegas archive facility, where they remain safe. Some of Shari's material is also at the UCLA Film and Television Archive.

All these years later, the question is: Could Shari Lewis make it in today's quick-paced, slang-using, product-savvy world of children's television? "Yes, I think she could," says Kids First's Ranny Levy, who cites reports that millennials think modern technology makes it harder to relate to people on a personal level. "What does this have to do with Shari? It's how people interact with each other and their communities. We *are* humans, you know, and if you look at what Shari did and her personality on her show, whether it was herself speaking or her speaking through the puppet, she is completely engaging and entertaining. Could you do the same thing with animation? You could try, but it wouldn't have the same feeling through it. I'm not a researcher or a scientist, but we connect with human beings in a human way. It's why animated violence is considered acceptable to a lot of people because it's 'just animation.'"

Shawn Williamson has a somewhat different view. "Half-hour children's shows now exist, but there's more animation than there was then, and puppetry is a bit, I think, of a dying art on television just because kids are seeing things that are photorealistic now. But I think that Shari would have adapted to whatever sold now because she was a brilliant performer and a brilliant writer and Lamb Chop certainly had legs, as it were. She would have found news ways of telling stories within that medium."

Gary H. Grossman, who chronicled the rise and fall of early children's television, laments, "It's a shame that Shari did not live to the time we're now in, with Netflix and Hulu and Amazon. She wouldn't be over-the-air, she'd be on the internet. And she would still be relevant."

"The beauty of her is that she was so low-tech," says Colman DeKay. "I don't know what kids would think about her these days. She was really of her time, wasn't she? She did reinvent herself a bunch, but it was always the basic simplicity of hand puppets. You'd have to find somebody with that skill, and that's hard."

Shari's legacy can be found not only in the work she left behind but also in her mentoring of three generations of viewers and coworkers. "The most important thing she taught me," says Williamson, who has gone on to produce hundreds of hours of television, "was never underestimate the importance of making people feel valued and part of a team, and remember that people matter, the movie doesn't matter. If people all sit together and work collaboratively, we'll make a great product. You trust the creative process but make sure people are valued. And that, for me, . . . was also a lesson that I use daily. Because, as producers, we do almost nothing. I'm being somewhat facetious, but compared to what the cast and the writers and the directors all do, they're working and pouring their heart and soul into what they're doing. My job is to make sure all those people have what they need to do their job in a safe, pleasant environment—and then they will succeed. Bernie [Rothman] and Shari sit with me daily in my career."

Shari Lewis was a survivor in a field that praised what she did yet threw obstacles in her path. Time after time, she vaulted over all of them. Her career, and the careers of others like her, beg the overriding question: Does television have a responsibility to children? Yes. But let's cut budgets so quality programming is sacrificed. Can the medium be used to teach critical thinking to its young viewers? Yes. But don't do it, or they won't grow up to be good consumers. Is it better for kids to be raised by humans and not by cartoons? Yes. But humans cost too much, so we'll settle for cartoons.

It took someone whose lips didn't move to survive all the lip service. More than what she said to her young viewers, Shari will be remembered for who she was. Not a parent, but a playmate. Not a teacher, but a big sister. Not a promise maker, but a promise keeper. She never just *said;* she *did.*

"I've never wanted to fit in," Shari once revealed. "I've never had any desire to be part of the group. I've always felt that I had to take care of myself, that nobody was gonna do anything for me. It makes for a very defensive personality but it also makes for a survival personality, 'cause the truth is that nobody is gonna do it for you if you don't do it for yourself. I'm interested in what people say," she went on. "I like one-on-one. A lady came up to me the other day and said, 'Are you the original Shari Lewis?' And I said to her, 'Yes, I am the original Shari Lewis—with most of the original parts!'"

16

Not Your Mother's Lamb Chop

When Shari died, she almost took Lamb Chop with her. Throughout their forty-year partnership, Shari had decreed that no one but she would be allowed to perform as her beloved puppet. But after Shari's death, Mallory picked up Lamb Chop. It was almost an afterthought. Or perhaps it was Fate. "My husband Brad was, in part, responsible for my continuing Lamb Chop," Mallory recounts. "The first year after Mom died, I was collecting posthumous awards pretty much every week. Brad said to me, 'You can't make a living collecting posthumous awards. Do you want to do her or not?' because I clearly liked the applause and I also couldn't imagine a world in which my little sister was dead. I figured I'd give it a shot."

The breakthrough happened at the Daytime Emmy® Awards. "Mallory and I went to the Daytime Emmys to accept [Shari's] award," Brad Hood says. "As we were leaving [the house], Mallory said, 'Do you think I should bring Lamb Chop?' She could do Lamb Chop really well. I said, 'Yeah, because we want to keep Lamb Chop alive. Lamb Chop's magic is still here. Why don't you just have her say something, anything.' And Mallory did. She had Lamb Chop say just a couple of words at the Emmys and it let everybody know that Lamb Chop was still there. All of a sudden we started getting calls to do shows."

Mallory turned down the first few offers, not having any material prepared, but then she decided to accept one, a Christmas show in Boston, as a test. Brad went through boxes and boxes of Shari's scripts and tapes to find the right material, and the result was a sensation. Lamb Chop was back, and she fit Mallory like a woolen glove. "What was funny," Brad says, "is that when we rehearsed the Christmas show, Mallory went to do a song with Lamb Chop. Well, Mallory needed some lessons, but Lamb Chop was pitch-perfect. Lamb Chop could sing really well."

"Lamb Chop would not be here today without Brad," says Mallory, who remains close to him even after the end of their thirteen-year marriage. In addition to finding material for her, Brad photographed Mallory's head shots and discovered, while printing them, that Shari, whose natural hair was dark brown, had dyed her hair red so as not to overpower the white-colored Lamb Chop in publicity photos. Mallory now dyes her hair red, too. Finally, Brad suggested that she change her professional name to Mallory Lewis. And then she was poifect. "There were three people who made it possible for me to take over Lamb Chop," Mallory says: "Stormy Sacks for the music, Pat Brymer for the puppets, and Brad Hood for all the other support. He also was and is an amazing dad, which, of course, made everything easier, and he continues to be a huge supporter of my performing efforts."

"In the big picture of things," says Todd Tillson, who watched the transition, "I didn't believe anybody could have carried on, but if somebody was going to, why not Mallory? What I didn't know—and was amazed by—was her ventricular [*sic*] abilities. When I first saw her show at the Magic Castle, I was amazed with her presence and performance."

Mallory's first step toward bringing Lamb Chop into modern times involved a dispassionate analysis of Shari's appeal, and it wasn't entirely based on ventriloquy. "A lot of guys come up to me now and tell me how they really loved my mom, and they'll be making those booby hands," she jokes, cupping her hands in front of her chest. "She wore a lot of tight sweaters. Essentially, I curate the show. Of the hour I'm onstage, for thirty minutes I'm performing with Lamb Chop. We do some songs, then I cue the video of my mother's highlights. I come back again and we do some more songs, and I cue more video. It's back and forth; I know everybody is really there because they would like to see Mom. They're okay with me, but I tell them I know you wish it was Shari Lewis and Lamb Chop. I do too. I ask, 'Who here remembers when Mom had blond hair?' The older people raise their hands. I say, 'You had a black-and-white TV.' Then I go, 'Hands up for the ponytail. Who here remembers the shag? How about the pageboy? Tight curls?' Then I go, 'Who here remembers the curls in back?' That's the *Charlie Horse Music Pizza* kids. I can tell which decade by which hairdo. Everybody gets to see a memory that they remember."

The result of this audience interaction—which Shari seldom engaged in—has given Mallory perspective. "Why is Lamb Chop valid after sixty years? Because she's funny, and kids don't change. The medium in which they get their entertainment may be different, but they still like silly and warm and genuine. Mom survived by always being relevant. I ask if there are any *Star Trek* fans in the audience. I say she and Dad wrote a *Star Trek* [episode]. It's the second coolest thing they did—after making me. I have a four-minute clip that's all pop culture things, including Lamb Chop with the doctor (Fred Gwynne). Then I close with 'Hello-Goodbye' and we're done."

Mallory continues her mother's legacy in public, but in private she has lived quite a life of her own. "I was born July 8, 1962, unless you read my Facebook page, which says 1972," she says, launching into a refreshingly frank reminiscence. "I knew that if I took off ten years, I could remember and always subtract ten."

Shari and Mallory bonded early, but more as friends than as mother and daughter. "My mom was not particularly interested in having a child," Mallory admits, "but children's entertainers of that era had to have a child. My father was totally disinterested in raising a child, but I was very lucky; I had lovely nannies and my mom was a dedicated, if not enthusiastic, parent." As a result, mother and daughter came to an understanding. A prime example was the Girl Scouts, which Mallory joined and then volunteered her mother as troop leader. "This lasted until one day when I realized that, if the troop meeting's always at your house, you have to help clean up afterwards, and I had no interest in that. The uniforms were also atrocious. Finally, after one meeting, Mom said, 'I'm only doing this for you,' and I said, 'Well, *I'm* only doing this for *you*,' and she said, 'Well, let's stop,' and I said, 'Okay.'" So much for Girl Scouts.

It didn't take Mallory long to realize that she was a handful. Precocious, noncompliant, and determined, she found that, like many only children, she related more easily to adults than to her peers. In fact, "I was completely disinterested in other kids my age and in school," she says. "My mom wanted a good student, but a planet can only revolve around one sun, and the planet of our family revolved around the sun of my mother."

Shari employed a succession of nannies to raise Mallory during the infant and toddler stage, when television kept her away from the house during the day. "I remember, at one point, she had fired the nanny, or the nanny had left, and I was upset about it—I was about eight—and Mom said, 'You can't get attached to the help.' I remember thinking to myself, 'Well who the hell am I *supposed* to get attached to?' But again, the judgments that people place on mothers are far more strict than the judgments they place on fathers, which is completely unfair."

When Shari was compelled to reinvent herself for the grown-up market in the early 1970s, she found her daughter to be a boon traveling companion. Between Mallory's classes at Hawthorne Elementary School, they lived the peripatetic life, going off together for Shari's club engagements. "She was really fun to travel with," Mallory says. "When we were in Vegas we would get up around eleven, we would have breakfast or lunch, and then go do a fun kid thing like the car museum; her favorite car was the 1929 Blond Thomas. Then we would go back to the hotel and take a nap, and then we would cut through the back hallways of the casino and I would sit backstage . . . and watch her show . . . , and then we would go to the coffee shop at one o'clock in the morning, when her shows were done, and play keno while we had our late-night snack, and then, you know, rinse, repeat."

By comparison, school was an exercise in boredom. "I hated it," Mallory says. One reason for her antipathy was that Shari didn't seem to care about it either. "She didn't come to school events, so I had very little interest in school because it clearly wasn't anything that the family had any interest in—except for when my report cards came in, and then it was a great disappointment. As an only child, you learn to read early. I loved reading and spent a lot of time in the world of books. I was definitely not the right child for my parents."

And yet, remembers Mallory, "we had a wonderful time doing fairs together. As I got older, Mom would let me bring a friend. She was, I think, the second or third act at Disney World. As I got older she would also say to the guy who was running the fair, 'I need a thirteen-year-old to go around with my nine-year-old and make sure she's okay.' We would always have a golf cart and be able to cut in line. There was a lot of fun."

When I'm at a performance venue, the one thing I'm very careful about is whether my mike pack is on. One time Mom was doing a big show, and at intermission she went backstage to pee. The sound guy hadn't turned off her mike, and the entire audience of ten thousand people heard my mother urinating. That made a big impression on me.
—*Mallory*

Mallory weighs her words, and the messages are mixed, to say the least. "I mean, she didn't do anything *wrong.* She was ultimately herself, so"—there is a long pause—"I don't know how to explain it except that, I mean, even the things I am saying that people don't know about Mom are not criticisms. She was a good mom. She just wasn't genuinely interested in momming. She made sure I had everything I needed." She corrects herself quickly: "No. She made sure I had everything she *thought* I needed. That would be the best way to put it. But, you know, as parents, we all do the best we can."

Before Mallory was school age, the Tarchers lived on the Upper West Side of New York at Ninety-Sixth and Riverside. They relocated to Beverly Hills in 1967, when Mallory was five. After Hawthorne, Mallory attended Beverly Hills High School, where the children of famous parents were inevitably enrolled. "I was not the right girl for Beverly Hills," she says sarcastically, referring to both the town and the famous educational institution. "The girls were bitches. Plus I was really small, and it's not like now with kids' clothes that look like little mini-adult clothes. Mine looked like little children's clothes, and I was twelve years old wearing clothes the size of an eight-year-old. Beverly Hills was very fashion oriented. I had no interest in the other kids and they had no interest in me."

Dating started at age fifteen. "Boys have always liked me," she says. "Michael Lawrence, Steve Lawrence and Eydie Gormé's son, was my first lover." It mattered not that she was the daughter of Shari Lewis and the sister of Lamb Chop; Beverly Hills High School was a tough room. "It was Roger Moore's daughter I was in school with, Shirley Jones's kid Patrick Cassidy I was in school with. It was Chuck Barris's daughter, Greg Morris's daughter, George Schlatter's daughter—my mom was not terribly famous compared with the other parents. Also, that was during Mom's least famous time. At Beverly Hills High School we were lower-middle-class celebrities."

Astonishingly, despite a lack of grades, Mallory got into Barnard College. "The reason I got into Barnard was that I had really great SATs. My grade point average was about a 3.2, but during admissions season, Mom waited until she was in the White House to call the Admissions Office to find out about my application. The admissions counselor answered the phone and heard, 'This is the White House operator calling for Shari Lewis.' So I got in. Shades of *Varsity Blues*!" But, she notes, "It was the wrong school for me. I was not a student. That's a school where people go who know how to study, so it took me five years to get through." Meanwhile, during a summer sojourn in England, she met a man named Gordon Lamb (remember that name).

After barely graduating, Mallory went to work in the fast-growing home video industry. "My first job was as the eastern regional sales manager for New World Pictures. This was right when the question was VHS or Beta. It was a great job, but during my personnel interview the guy said, 'Why should I hire you if you have no experience?' I said, 'Well, you *want* to hire me, don't you?' and he said, 'Yes.' I said, 'Well, obviously I can sell.' Later I went into RCA/Columbia Pictures home video, and then I came home. It was the 1980s. I needed to come home."

When Mallory was twenty-five, she married Michael Doherty. "I met him at a publishing convention," she says. "He was a very nice man, a publicist. And then I came home." Like her mother, she dismisses her first marriage (it ended when she was twenty-seven) and moves the conversation to another subject.

Now Gordon Lamb comes back into the picture. "Gordon and I met when I was in England the summer I was eighteen," she says, "and he was a top horse trainer. We became best friends and he came to America to live with me when I was in college, since I wasn't going to class anyway." The two of them shared her dorm room at Barnard while he traveled back and forth to Europe and she pretended to work on a degree. According to Lamb, "I lived with Mallory, then I moved to [Greenwich] Village, then I went back to Europe, then back to LA and decided I wanted to live with her, so I stayed and we lived together for a while, and then I did my thing teaching riding, and she was doing her thing, and then she met [Michael] and she got married and I went back to Europe again, and then I came back again like a bad penny."

According to Mallory, "When I finished my marriage to Michael, I remember saying to Gordon, 'Look, why don't *we* get married? Let's do it now, 'cause I shouldn't marry anyone else for three years anyway. I need to get my head together.'" Mallory and Gordon got married in either 1992 or 1993 (both of them are vague). This entitled Lamb to a green card, and he worked part time for Shari as a production assistant and occasional driver while *Lamb Chop's Play-Along* was in production. "Nothing glamorous," he says. "Shari knew about us so we were close but not like kin or something. Kind of weird. But I really loved Shari. Shari was a cool person. She wasn't what I thought she was going to be, and what I mean by that is that I sort of grew up with Shari on TV in England. She was very talented and smart and we had lots of great conversations."

Lamb watched Mallory change from an unsure eighteen-year-old into a woman who knows her own mind and freely shares it. "She's a different person now," he says, "but I am, too. We're both kind of outsiders. She was an only child and her mother and father were working professionals. She was obviously indulged. I was a middle child and my folks were always off doing their own thing too. We're kindred spirits in that way. When I met her, we were both so young. She'd drive her mother crazy. She would do stuff just to get noticed. The thing is, she's a really good person. We've all pissed off people in our lives, of course, but with all that, she's a much nicer person than me." Their divorce in 1996 didn't end their friendship. "We get on with our lives," Lamb says, "but we're always there for each other. It's a weirdly close relationship." The two are still close, and Lamb gave Mallory her most recent horse, Abe, an Arabian that looks very similar to Oliver, the horse on which Gordon schooled her in England decades previously.

Then Mallory's life took another turn—or, rather, descent. "I was on the set when a man named Ken Cathro started mentioning skydiving. I said, 'Oh, I'd like to try that.' My mom said, '*I absolutely forbid it!*' And of course that weekend I went and jumped out of a plane. I hated the plane ride, I hated the exit, I hated free fall, I hated the canopy ride, I hated the landing. And the first words out of my mouth were, 'Great buzz! Can I do it again?'"

After ending her marriage with Lamb, Mallory took the plunge (sorry), with fellow skydiver Brad Hood. "One year after I started skydiving I met my baby-daddy and longest-term husband," she says. "He was a skydiving cinematographer, one of the best in the world." Their meeting had echoes of Jeremy's first meeting with Shari. "I was filming a commercial at a big drop zone and Mallory was friends with the owners," Brad says. "I'm giving a safety briefing to all the department heads. We get started and Mallory just kind of bursts through the door and she's got a bag of McDonald's breakfast and she goes, 'Oh!' She wanted to be in this meeting, so she just came in. That was my introduction to her. She was on the commercial, of course, and we made some plans to get together after the commercial, and one thing led to another. We decided to go out and have coffee or do something, and I said, 'When are you available?' I thought she would say, 'Next week.' She pulled a date two months away. I was shocked and said, 'Oh, okay,' and we parted ways with me thinking she had blown me off. Who does that? Who says 'six weeks from now'?" He smiles at the answer: "Her mother."

As their romance developed on land and in the air, it was in fact Shari's favor that Brad had to win. His first meeting with her happened in July 1992 at Mallory's birthday party slash housewarming. "She had just acquired a house in the Valley and we had just started dating," Brad says. "So I show up and, no, it's not just a little birthday party. It's catered, there's a bar set up in the backyard with guys in penguin suits, everybody's all decked out. It's all these Hollywood people. Now I'm having to meet everyone in the family, everyone in the industry, as Mallory's new boyfriend. That was the first day. Shari did attack me a few times."

"Mom initially didn't want to like Brad," Mallory says, "because he wasn't Jewish and he wasn't a doctor and she knew he was the man I was going to reproduce with. She wanted me to reproduce with a Jewish doctor. A lawyer would also have been fine. She actually, once, at the very beginning of our relationship, sent her hairdresser over—Brad had a broken leg and he needed a haircut—she sent her hairdresser over, ostensibly to cut Brad's hair, but actually to check if that blond was his natural color. She couldn't believe how beautiful his hair was and assumed he was dyeing it! By the end, she recognized what a quality human being my future husband was."

"First Shari tried to get rid of me because I didn't meet her standards," Brad says, "but she had a saying, 'If there is no solution, there is no problem.' I think, eventually, they figured out there was no solution for me, so then I became the greatest skydiver in the world, better than anybody else, and that's kinda how we left it."

"Once she decided if there is no solution there is no problem," Mallory adds, "she allowed herself to be open. I always thought it was really sweet that Brad never held her initial unpleasantness against her."

The wedding was held December 27, 1997, in their home in Van Nuys. "It was just my mom and my dad and Brad's mom and dad and Georgia. We had a big party at the Museum of Flight in Santa Monica with a hundred people. We had the best exit ever. Brad and I were skydiving professionally at the time, and the man who owned the helicopter company he worked with said, 'I'd really like you to work with me more,' so, as a freebie, they said they would fly and land at the Museum of Flight and take us away and fly us to LAX, where we were [leaving for] our honeymoon."

Their son James Abraham Tarcher Hood was born on February 27, 1999. The marriage lasted until 2011. Says Mallory, "We dated and married and I had Jamie and we had a fairly successful marriage that lasted thirteen years, and then didn't." Nevertheless, Mallory is quick to add, "We have co-parented perfectly. He's at dinner every couple of weeks

Mom performed at my school. She did the Christmas show, usually. All my friends at my school knew my mom, and they still ask about her. I probably asked her to stop doing it, but four or five years later they still say, "How's your mom?" There were plenty of times when we were at fairs, meeting all these people. She would bite the bullet and she would get sick—you can't avoid it—but she would never not interact with me. She drove me to kindergarten, did times tables with me in the car every day. She was doing all her shows and things, but I was never backseat to Lamb Chop or the show or any of that.

—*Jamie Hood*

whether Jamie's home or not. Dear friends we will always be. There's no drama; it's just the best possible solution."

While Jamie was growing up, Mallory made it a point to perform at his school with Lamb Chop. Jamie never knew his Grandma Shari. The closest he came was being inside Mallory during the shooting of *The Charlie Horse Music Pizza*. But he was raised watching Shari's videos and grew close to the woman whose embrace he would never feel. "Jamie was two, two and a half," Mallory recalls. "I came into his room and he said, 'Grandma Shari was here last night.' I said, 'Oh, you had a dream about her?' He said, 'No, Mommy, she was *here*.' I said, 'Oh, okay.' And then, when he was only slightly older than that, he drew a picture of my mom and I said, 'Oh, Grandma Shari would have liked that.' And he ran out into the backyard, held the picture up to the sky, came back, and said, 'She loves it.'"

Granted, very young children cannot differentiate between fantasy and reality, but according to Mallory, Jamie was ahead of the maturity curve. "I was editing some videos I had done. He was five, sitting on the couch. As we had already shown these videos, he knew that I had done a song about a ball. He looked at me and said, 'Put this in the same episode as the game about the ball.' I looked at him and I said, 'Yes, Shari!' and he turned his little five-year-old head to me, winked one eye, and looked back at the TV. Another time we were editing and he said, 'Get out before your smile fades.' Now that's really weird, because at the end of a song you're smiling, and then you stop. Literally, I would get notes from Mom that said, 'Get out before my smile fades.' Here a five-year-old says it. He has her eyes and he has her soul."

Now twenty-three and a graduate with a master's degree from the Georgetown School of Foreign Service in Washington, DC, Jamie is keeping his career options open, with one exception: no show business. He scrubbed that from his dance card after years of touring with his parents whenever school vacations and weekends allowed, although he jumps in to help his mom when his schedule permits. "I started [doing sound for Mallory's shows] when I was about eight," Jamie says. "I would be in the sound area where we were running everything with my dad, and he would run it for the first seven or eight years. The first time I did it, it was the show in New York. Mom had a guy who was going to come in

> I was brought up in LA my whole life, in the industry, and people ask, "Do you go to Hollywood? Do you see movie stars?" Living here, it's local; you see it for what it is. I wanted to go to DC to have a local's knowledge of politics—living and breathing knowledge, not just what I see on TV.
>
> —*Jamie Hood*

and do the sound, but his car ran off the road (snowstorm, winter) so we didn't have anyone to do sound. I managed to do it that time, and from then on, it was a sink-or-swim moment."

"When Jamie was born, we incorporated him into the act," says Brad. "We were doing a lot of USO shows, we were doing performing arts centers, one pretty consistent gig doing pre-luau shows over in Hawaii, and that was fun. Eventually the USO thing—we went to Texas, we went all over the United States—and took Jamie right along with us. When he was little he would fall asleep on top of the big giant speaker at shows. When he got to be eight years old or so, he would sit with me, all three of us would go to the show, and Mallory would be onstage and I would be wherever we could set the equipment, so Jamie would hang out with me the same way Mallory would hang out with her father, Jeremy, when Shari would do the shows."

"I did most of my work with Mom on summer tours, on the fair tours," Jamie says. "They even took me in a little bucket when I was a baby. We'd spend a month during the summer doing Wisconsin, Ohio, Iowa, back-to-back. It would be three shows a day, fourteen days in a row. That was when I was ten or eleven. I was doing all the setups and Mom was doing all the magic. I still call a few shows a year; sometimes she flies me out to wherever she is because from DC it's pretty easy to commute to places if I have to."

> Of course I played with them and slept with Lamb Chop when I was little, and I'm protective of Lamb Chop. I was always heir to the behind-the-scenes stuff, but I'm not really an entertainer.
>
> —*Jamie Hood*

Growing up in a show-business family hardened Jamie to the glamor of Hollywood (although, like his mother, he has a sweet spot for *Star Trek*). What insulates him from being known as Lamb Chop's kid brother is that his peers didn't grow up with the puppets. "Sometimes I meet people that know Lamb Chop," he says. "It gets confusing when people ask, 'What does your mom do?' and I always know they won't quite get it. But sometimes I say, 'Your parents will know.' But no one in my age group does. Sometimes their parents will show them; they grew up on it and want it to be part of their [kids'] upbringing. But it hasn't been on the air in my whole lifetime, twenty years now."

Jamie was twelve when his parents split, and Mallory held off forming any long-term relationships. "I didn't want to have a significant relationship while my child was living at home with me," she says. Once Jamie headed off to Georgetown, however, "I did what my mother would have suggested: I joined the tennis club and met a nice man there." But no sparks. "Maybe a month later I was at the American Airlines lounge on Christmas Day and I saw this devastatingly handsome man wearing the most absurd Christmas tie ever. I went over to him and I said, 'Nice tie.' He said, 'Thank you.' I said, 'Why are you in a suit on Christmas Day?' And he said, 'T.W.B.' I said, 'What does that mean?' He said, 'Traveling While Black. It goes better in a suit.' I was in ripped jeans, a white shirt, and a massive Hermes scarf, and I said, 'I'm T.W.J.' He said, 'What does that mean?' I said, 'Traveling While Jewish. We don't give a shit.' We started to laugh and I said, 'What's your name?' He said, 'Brian Cummings.' I said my name and asked, 'What do you do?' 'Well, I'm a retired firefighter.' We flirted and exchanged numbers, and when he left, I Googled him. And I was so impressed. He said he was a retired firefighter; what he was was the retired fire chief for the City of Los Angeles. I thought that was such an elegant undersell. It took us three weeks to go out because of our varying schedules, but we started dating and it was pretty instant for both of us. We got married on the day of New Year's Eve, December 31, 2018, and so far have been living happily ever after. I feel incredibly lucky that my husband, Brian, my ex-husband, Brad, and my son, Jamie, and I are all dear friends. We support and love and enjoy each other as a family."

It was Brian's second marriage and Mallory's fourth. Brian is Catholic and Mallory is a self-proclaimed Jewish atheist. They were joined in a

Jewish ceremony performed by a rabbi she had met on a ski trip to Deer Valley. She knew he was right for the job "because he ran a ski shul." While some rabbis might have balked at officiating at a mixed marriage, this one said, "Tell me how you two feel about religion." Mallory replied, "It's a crock of shit, I don't believe in God, but I'm very culturally Jewish." Brian said, "I'm Catholic and I believe in everything, all of it." The rabbi said, "Well, as long as you don't have kids, it should be fine."

Shortly before their marriage, Brian had to call on his experience to protect his and Mallory's new home in Malibu. It was November 9, 2018, when Malibu experienced some of the worst infernos in Southern California history. "The fires crested the hill and he sent me away," Mallory reports. "So I went up to Santa Barbara to Bacara because, if you have to go someplace, it might as well be a spa, and he stayed and fought the fire. I have these fabulous pictures and videos of him laughing and enjoying himself in full fireman regalia. He saved our house, and then he and our neighbor Fred and our neighbor Matty, the three of them together, saved a number of houses in the area. The fire stopped *one foot from our property.* It would have burned the house, except Brian put it out."

Mallory recalls, "I'd been hearing from Brian all day, but I hadn't heard from my ex-husband, Brad. Jamie, who'd kept calling me, kept asking, 'Have you heard from Dad?' Brad runs a three hundred–acre ranch, and he's the kind of guy who'd stay to save it. I'd say to Jamie, 'Naw, Dad's fine,' and get more and more nervous. Finally the phone rings and it was Brad, and I said, 'Oh, thank God, are you okay?' and he said, 'Yes, but I don't want to grow up to be a fireman anymore.' He had no place to go because he couldn't get to his house, so he came and spent the night with Brian. They were sitting on the couch and Brad said, 'Chief, what time does the fire camp go to sleep?' It's very lovely because we are truly a blended family."

Currently, Brian is the fire tech adviser on Shonda Rhimes's hit TV series *Station 19*. After four seasons on the job, he's another member of Lamb Chop's family in show business.

If it sounds like the setup for a super-polite British drawing-room comedy, it isn't. It's the result of maturity and perspective. Lamb Chop must be very happy that, at age six going on sixtyish, she is once again working and living in a stable home. Shari has been gone twenty-three years.

And so the torch has passed, although it's not a torch—it's a sock with an attitude. Shari Lewis was a woman who ran her own business and her own life yet made time for family, friends, and the public. She had crushing lows and intoxicating highs but never forgot the wisdom of her father, who taught her that problems can be solved the same way you eat an elephant: one bite at a time. Shari climbed to the top of a profession that everybody said was dead even before she entered it. She made her own way, survived three generations of change, and left a legacy that her daughter now uses to create new memories for Shari's grown-up fans and their children.

"I was going to a gig in I think Milwaukee," Mallory said in 2016, "and they were going to do a whole display in tribute to Mom, and they were going to pay me extra. I said, 'Do you want me to ship you some of Mom's ashes?' They said, 'Nah, that's okay.' I said, 'Are you sure? She's been gone fourteen years, she'd love to have a gig.' Which I know to be true. I almost lost the gig out of sounding like a crazy person. I answered fan mail for her yesterday. She's been dead nineteen years and she still gets fan mail, and I still answer it. I think it's amazing that all these years after she's gone, people are still thinking of her."

Afterword

Lamb Chop Speaks

No biography of Shari Lewis would be complete without input from Lamb Chop. This was not an easy "get," as they say in the interview business, because she is a very busy six-year-old. But Mallory arranged for her to say a few words to her coauthor, Nat.

Nat: Can you find Lamb Chop?
Mallory: She said she'd be back by now. Hold on. She was at the gym. Here she is.
Lamb Chop: Hello, Nat.
Nat: Oh, by the way, may I have your permission to record this conversation?
Lamb Chop: Of course.
Nat: No, I need Mallory's permission. She's an adult and you're only six.
Mallory: Yes.
Nat: Hi, Lammie. It's so good to talk to you. It's been a long time.
Lamb Chop: You never call, that's why!
Nat: What's the difference between working with Shari and working with Mallory?
Lamb Chop: Well, that's an easy one. Shari was my mom, and so I respected her and I trusted her and I counted on her good judgment. Mallory is not my mom; she's my little sister. So there.
Nat: How do you manage to keep your act fresh all these years?
Lamb Chop: You know, I stay on social media and try to keep up with the trends.
Nat: If you were speed-dating, how would you describe yourself to a potential partner?
Lamb Chop: Eighteen inches of hubba-hubba.

Nat: What do you think of the way children's television has changed since you started working in it?
Lamb Chop: I think it sucks cuz I'm not on it.
Nat: Can you elaborate? Were there favorite people you used to watch when you were little?
Lamb Chop: Well, when I was little I was the biggest star in television. But I was a big fan of the Beatles and the Monkees and I'm dating myself by saying those are my favorites.
Nat: Oh, you're eternal, Lamb Chop. I don't think you have to worry about dating yourself, ever.
Lamb Chop: *Enchanté.*
Nat: How do children react when they meet you versus how adults react when they meet you?
Lamb Chop: Children squeal and giggle and the grown-ups cry cuz they miss me.
Nat: Of all the celebrities you've worked with such as Dom DeLuise, Margaret Hamilton, Fred Gwynne, and more, who was the most fun to work with?
Lamb Chop: Mallory.
Nat: Okay, she's a star, but I mean the people who were just day players.
Lamb Chop: Dean Martin. Cuz he was really sexy.
Nat: How would you describe your relationship with Charlie Horse and Hush Puppy?
Lamb Chop: Charlie Horse and Hush Puppy are my big brothers and Hush Puppy is the sweet one and Charlie Horse is [pause] not the sweet one.
Nat: Did you ever get to meet Wing Ding, Taffy Twinkle, Samson, or any of Shari's other puppets?
Lamb Chop: I did. We were all shoved into a suitcase together once.
Nat: How would you like to be remembered?
Lamb Chop: As the cutest, biggest, longest-lasting star of all time.
Nat: Okay, here's a tough one. Now that Shari is gone, what did you really think of her?
Lamb Chop: I thought she was a really nice lady who always took really good care of me and was really pretty. She was my best friend and I miss her . . . but luckily I get to watch her on YouTube!
Nat: Thank you, Lamb Chop. It was wonderful talking to you, and I didn't see your lips move once while Mallory was talking.

Appendix A

Shari's Favorite Lamb Recipes

"Lamb has been feeding our family for years," says Mallory with a smile as she pores through her mother's recipe file. No iPad here; like every woman of her era, housewife or not, Shari kept her recipes on three-by-five-inch cards in a little box in the kitchen. When Shari appeared in a cooking segment on a talk show, very often the host had her make one of her lamb dishes. At home, though, it was housekeeper Georgia Anderson who did the cooking, no doubt fine-tuning Shari's recipes to make them work (because some of them, judging by the cards, are incomplete at best). These recipes have not been tested (not at the price of lamb these days!), so try them at your own risk.

Barbecued Leg of Lamb

1 6-lb leg of lamb, boned and flattened (butterflied)
1 cup oil
¼ cup wine vinegar
2 garlic cloves, crushed
1 tablespoon salt
Freshly ground black pepper
Hot barbecue sauce

Marinate lamb at room temperature for 2 hours in oil, vinegar, garlic, salt, and pepper. Turn the lamb once or twice and baste occasionally with the marinade. Remove from marinade and broil for 2 hours or until done,* turning frequently and basting with hot barbecue sauce.

**This is more properly called a butterflied leg of lamb. If you broil the lamb for 2 hours, you'll end up with a slab of charcoal. Instead, broil it 6 inches from the* *flame for 12 to 16 minutes, then turn it over, brush with barbecue sauce, and broil on the second side for another 12 to 16 minutes, depending on the desired doneness. Allow the lamb to rest for 5 minutes before carving at an angle.*

Barbecued Lamb Marinade*

Cut up leg of lamb into small pieces. Marinate in mixture of oil, red [?] and vinegar (more vinegar), garlic, mint, salt & pepper for 1/2 days. On spear, put cubes of meat, alternate with cubes of pepper, onion, tomatoes. Barbecue about 25 minutes. Turn skewer and baste as you go.

**This isn't a marinade recipe; it's a recipe for skewered lamb, or lamb kabobs, that have been marinated. It's meant to be cooked on a grill.*

Curried Lamb

3 pounds lamb shoulder or neck
¼ cup flour
2 garlic cloves, minced
4 large onions, sliced
¾ cup butter
4 small apples, pared and chopped
4 tablespoons curry powder
4 tablespoons brown sugar
4 tablespoons raisins
2 tablespoons Worcestershire sauce
2 lemons, sliced
4 tablespoons shredded coconut
¾ cup chopped walnuts
½ teaspoon grated lime peel
1 tablespoon salt

Cut meat into 2-inch cubes. Roll it in flour. Sauté garlic and onions and butter in large skillet for 5 minutes or until lightly browned. Add meat and sauté for normal 10 minutes, stirring constantly. Add apples and curry powder. Simmer for 5 minutes, stirring occasionally. Add the remaining ingredients and 2 cups of water. Bring to a boil, reduce heat, cover and simmer for 1 hour. Serves 6. Beef, veal, or pork can be used instead of lamb. Fresh or leftover peas, string or wax beans, carrot slices, mushrooms, or quarters of green pepper may be added to curry during the last 10 minutes of cooking.

Grilled Leg of Lamb (Bouti Arni-Skaras)

1 6- to 7-pound leg of lamb
Salt, pepper
½ cup olive oil
Juice of 1 lemon
2 teaspoons crushed dried oregano

Rinse a leg of lamb and pat dry. Trim off any excess fat. Season to taste with salt and pepper. To cook meat over indirect heat, use a long-handled fork to move hot coals to outer edges of the barbecue and place a drip pan underneath grill. Place lamb, fat side down, on grill and cook 30 minutes.

Meanwhile, combine olive oil, lemon juice, and oregano in small bowl. Baste lamb, turn over, and baste again. Cover and cook about 1½ hours longer, basting 2 or 3 times. Meat thermometer should read 145 degrees for medium-rare or 160 for well-done. Let stand 20 minutes before carving. Makes 8 servings.

Lamb Stew

2 tbs olive oil
1 onion, chopped
2 cloves of garlic, minced
1 pound lamb shoulder cut into 1-inch cubes
3 cups chicken broth
2 sliced carrots
1 rib celery, chopped
½ cup green onion

In a large pot, heat 2 tablespoons of olive oil and sauté 1 chopped medium onion and 2 minced cloves of garlic until translucent. And 1 lb. lamb shoulder cut into 1-inch cubes and another 2 tablespoons olive oil. Sauté lamb until lightly browned. Add 3 cups chicken broth, two sliced carrots, one chopped rib celery, ½ cup chopped green onion. Bring to boil, reduce heat, and simmer until lamb is tender, about 1 hour, skimming any foam from surface. Season to taste with salt and pepper. Serves four.

Sausalito Lamb & Tortellini

(*Prep time: 15 min.*)
32 ounces boneless American lamb, cut in thin strips
Non-stick spray coating
¼ teaspoon garlic powder
1 can (14.5 ounces) Italian seasoned and diced tomatoes
1 can (8 ounces) low-sodium tomato sauce
½ cup beef broth
1 package (16 ounces) frozen mixed vegetables
1 package (9 ounces) refrigerated cheese tortellini*
Parmesan cheese, grated

Spray skillet with non-stick spray. Stir-fry lamb strips over high heat until browned. Remove from heat. Stir in all remaining ingredients except Parmesan. Return to heat; bring to boil. Reduce heat, cover, simmer 10 minutes. Stir once or twice. Sprinkle with Parmesan. Serves 4 to 6.

**The tortellini must be fresh, not dried, and should be cooked in the simmering liquid. This makes a substantial meal.*

Fresh Herb Marinade for Lamb

4 tablespoons lemon juice
4 tablespoons olive oil
1 tablespoon dark soy sauce
½ teaspoon of salt
Sweet-n-Low (a little)
2 to 3 garlic cloves, crushed
1 tablespoon chopped fresh thyme
1 tablespoon chopped fresh mint

Mix all ingredients and use to marinate lamb leg, steaks, or butterflied lamb leg.

Lamb Sauce

Fresh garlic
Green onions
Drawn butter
Shallots

In a blender and you keep the basting all through the cooking dash of salt & pepper.*

**This is all it says on Shari's recipe card. It seems best served on the side, or perhaps in the trash.*

Hal's Lamb*

½ cup Dijon type prepared mustard
1 tablespoon soy sauce
1 clove mashed garlic
1 teaspoon ground thyme
¼ teaspoon powdered ginger
2 tablespoons olive oil

Blend all except oil in bowl, beat in oil in droplets to make mayonnaise-like cream. Hours before roasting, paint on 6 pound leg of lamb and set on roast pan rack. Roast 350° for 1 to 1½ hours.

**We have no idea who Hal is, but his marinade is spicy and yields a piquant lamb.*

Lamb with Spinach from Punjab

3 pounds lean lamb, cut into 2½-inch cubes
1½ pounds spinach, cut in quarter inch strips
3 onions, thinly sliced
6 tablespoons butter
1½ teaspoons ground turmeric
1 tablespoon coriander seed
4 teaspoons ground ginger
¾ teaspoon chili powder
3 tablespoons yogurt
¼ teaspoon thyme
4 teaspoons mustard seed
1 teaspoon salt

Sauté onions in butter. Add meat, turmeric, coriander, ginger, and chili powder and simmer for 10 minutes. Stir in spinach, yogurt, thyme, mustard seeds, and salt. Cover and simmer for 15 minutes, stirring occasionally. Add ¼ cup water and simmer for 15 minutes. Serves six.

Mustard Roast Lamb

½ cup Dijon type mustard
2 tablespoons soy sauce
1 clove garlic, minced
1 teaspoon thyme
2 tablespoons oil
1 5 to 6 pound leg of lamb

Blend mustard seed with soy sauce until smooth. Stir in garlic and thyme. Gradually beat in oil until smooth. Brush mustard mixture on lamb. Place lamb on rack in shallow pan and let stand in refrigerator several hours. Roast at 325° until meat thermometer inserted in thickest part of leg registers 175°—about 2½ hours. Makes 6 to 8 servings.

Mustard Roast Lamb—Special Instructions

Make up five times recipe for the mustard sauce—put some in a jar, and give it to the butcher the next time he delivers meat.* Ask him to bone the leg of lamb, and spread this mustard sauce on the inside of the lamb before he rolls it up.

Then, after you have mustarded the outside of the lamb as well, shake bread crumbs (Italian flavored ones) over all the mustard.

When the lamb is done, pour off the juice. When cold, scoop away the hard fat, and the next time you heat the slices of the lamb, heat them with this juice.

**We love the phrase "give it to the butcher the next time he delivers meat." Talk about the old days. Shari had a fondness for mustard and lamb (see also below) but, curiously, no interest in traditional mint jelly, despite her punch line to the waiter (see chapter 12).*

Grill Leg of Lamb with Mustard-Orange Sauce

1 6- to 7-pound full-cut leg of lamb, trimmed and butterflied
Oil
1 teaspoon rosemary
Salt
Freshly ground black pepper
½ cup butter or margarine
Zest and juice of 2 oranges
3 to 4 tablespoons Dijon mustard

Rub lamb all over with oil and sprinkle with rosemary. Season to taste with salt and pepper. Place lamb on grill fat side up over coals or on oven broiler pan, skin side away from heat source. Broil 6 inches from heat source 20 minutes. Turn lamb over and broil about 15 minutes longer. Lamb will be pink but not rare inside.

While lamb is broiling, melt the butter in small saucepan and stir in orange zest and juice and mustard. Simmer a few minutes, until mixture is slightly thickened.

When lamb is done, remove immediately to platter and pour sauce over. Let stand in warm spot 10 minutes before carving. Spoon sauce that accumulates in bottom of platter over meat several times during standing. To serve, cut in thin slices and spoon some of the sauce over each serving. Makes about 12 servings.

Leg of Lamb en Crute

3–4 pound leg of lamb or lamb shanks, boned
2 lamb kidneys
2 tbs butter or margarine
2 tbs Madeira wine
1 cup mushrooms
Thyme, rosemary, tarragon
Flaky pastry mix

Have your butcher bone shank end of a small leg of lamb (will weigh 3 to 4 pounds). Cube two lamb kidneys and sauté in skillet with 2 tablespoons of butter (or margarine). Add 2 tablespoons of Madeira wine, 1 cup cut fresh mushrooms (or well-drained canned), plus thyme, rosemary, and tarragon. Cook kidney and mushroom stuffing one or two minutes, fill hole where bone was removed; mold leg into shape, stitch or tie with heavy thread. Rub lamb with butter (or margarine), sear 15 minutes in preheated 450° F oven to seal in juices. Remove lamb, wrap in thinly rolled flaky pastry (mix or own recipe). Brush pastry with lightly beaten egg yolk; bake 40 minutes more. Serve with French mustard. Serves six.

Spicy Butterfly Leg of Lamb

Marinate ½ small lemon, finely chopped
Freshly ground black pepper
1 teaspoon ground allspice
1 teaspoon curry powder
1 teaspoon lemon juice
1 tablespoon sweet chili sauce (Thai style)
Sweet-n-Low or 1 tablespoon liquid honey
1 tablespoon oil

Mix marinade ingredients, spread on boned surfaces, leave lightly covered in a cool place for an hour or two. Barbecue over steady heat, skin side down to start, small leg 30 minutes, large 40 minutes. Turn lamb after 15 minutes, baste with oil during cooking. Allow meat to stand for 10 minutes before carving across grain.

Greek Meatballs with Lemon Sauce

1 pound ground lamb
1 cup chopped parsley
½ cup chopped onion
½ cup cooked rice
1 egg, beaten
1 teaspoon salt
¼ teaspoon pepper
2 cups beef bouillon
2 tablespoons cornstarch
3 tablespoons water
3 tablespoons lemon juice

Equipment: bowl; spoon; measuring cup and spoons; knife; large skillet with cover; egg beater.

Mix first 7 ingredients in bowl. Shape into 1½-inch balls. Bring bouillon to a boil in skillet, add meatballs. Cover; simmer 30 minutes. Remove meatballs to platter. Skim excess fat from broth. In bowl, mix cornstarch and water; stir into broth. Stirring constantly, bring to boil over medium heat and boil 1 minute. Add lemon juice and pour sauce over meatballs. Daisy.*

**Shari wrote "Daisy" at the end of the recipe. We have no idea who Daisy is. Maybe she and Hal were an item (see earlier recipe).*

Appendix B

Awards and Recognitions

- 13 Emmy Awards (1 posthumous), 4 other nominations
- Peabody Award (1960)
- 7 Parents' Choice Awards
- Action for Children's Television Award
- Entertainer of the Year, American Academy of Children's Entertainment (1995)
- Monte Carlo Prize for the World's Best Television Variety Show (1963)
- John F. Kennedy Center Award for Excellence and Creativity (1983)
- B'nai B'rith Dor L'Dor Award (1996)
- 3 Houston Film Festival Awards
- Silver Circle Award, National Academy of Television Arts and Sciences (1996)
- Film Advisory Board Award of Excellence (1996)
- 2 Charleston Film Festival Gold Awards (1995)
- Houston World Festival Silver and Bronze Awards (1995)
- New York Film and Video Festival Silver Award (1995)
- Women in Film Lucy Award (1998, posthumous)

Appendix C

List of Interviews

The bulk of Shari Lewis's comments are drawn from her October 13, 1994, interview with Nat Segaloff. Sources for other comments are cited where they first appear. Interviews for the A&E *Biography* episode "Shari Lewis and Lamb Chop," not listed here, were collected in October 1994.

Brady, Mary Lou (August 24, 2017)
Brown, Ben and David (March 3, 2017)
Brown, Elinore and Ben (February 9, 2017)
Brymer, Pat (April 28, 2019)
Charmoli, Tony (January 10, 2019)
Daly, Deborah (October 9, 2019)
DeKay, Colman (October 4, 2019)
Ehrlich, Harriet (February 16, 2017)
Fox, Sonny (April 22, 2019)
Gordon, Sonny (May 7, 2019)
Grossman, Gary H. (April 29, 2017; April 19, 2019)
Hood, Brad (August 13, 2019)
Hood, Jamie (August 13, 2019)
Hubbs, Heidi (April 26, 2019)
Hymowitz, Gary (April 26, 2019)
Johnson, Jay (October 23, 2019)
Lamb, Gordon (October 28, 2019)
Lee, Ralph (September 25, 2019)
Levy, Ranny (April 8, 2019)

Lewis, Mallory (January 28, 2017; May 9, 2019; August 13, 2019)
Loesch, Margaret (June 5, 2019)
Miller, Susan (April 30, 2019)
Naxon, Elya (March 1, 2017)
O'Kun, Barbara (April 8, 2017)
O'Kun, Lan (April 8, 2017)
Proft, Pat (April 2, 2019)
Rhodes, Carla (June 8, 2019)
Rushnell, Squire (May 1, 2019)
Seymour, Richard (May 6, 2019)
Stein, Carl (August 1, 2019)
Sweazy, Lisa (May 6, 2019)
Tillson, Todd (April 22, 2019)
Wexler, Judy (May 29, 2019)
Williamson, Shawn (October 1, 2019)
Zalk, Bernice (February 15, 2017)

Index